best *of*

stitch

BAGS TO SEW

From the editors of *Stitch* magazine
Compiled by Tricia Waddell

INTERWEAVE.
interweave.com

TECHNICAL EDITOR FOR NEW CONTENT
Cheryl Johnson

COVER + INTERIOR DESIGN
Pamela Norman

PHOTOGRAPHER
Joe Hancock, unless otherwise noted

ILLUSTRATOR
Ann Swanson

PRODUCTION
Katherine Jackson

© 2013 Interweave Press LLC
Photography © 2012 Joe Hancock
All rights reserved.

Interweave Press LLC
A division of F+W Media, Inc
201 East Fourth Street
Loveland, CO 80537
interweave.com

Printed in China by RR Donnelley Shenzhen

Library of Congress Cataloging-in-Publication Data not available at time of printing.
ISBN 978-1-59668-602-1 (pbk.)
ISBN 978-1-59668-928-2 (PDF)

10 9 8 7 6 5 4 3 2 1

contents

introduction

Somehow, we never seem to have enough bags. Every outfit, occasion, and season seems to call for its own carry-all. What could be more fun or satisfying than creating a one-of-a-kind custom bag that can't be found in any store, coordinated perfectly with your outfit?

If you share our bag obsession, we know that in the following pages you will find a bag project (or two or three) that will be the perfect accessory to a favorite outfit. We've chosen our favorite bag designs from the pages of *Stitch,* along with five brand-new, never-before-published designs to entice you to start sewing right away.

Pretty patchwork bags that are great for stashbusting, bags featuring creative embellishments from appliqué to embroidery, bags made with a variety of clever construction techniques—they're all here, and every project has a unique design twist. You'll find a variety of sizes and shapes, including totes, messenger bags, clutches, coin purses, wallets, and more. No matter how much or how little time you have to sew, or your sewing skill level, you will find the perfect project.

To ensure your sewing success, check out the technique sidebars throughout the book, from tips for sewing leather to DIY felting, along with general bag construction tips and tricks and sewing basics. You'll also find all the full-size pattern pieces and templates on the full-size pattern insert pages bound into the book.

What are you waiting for? Let's sew!

Happy sewing,
The Editors of *Stitch*

...making the most of your stash....

pretty in patchwork

If you love color, print, and pattern, and have the fabric stash to prove it, then patchwork is your best friend. There are so many ways to creatively approach fabric piecing. Showcase big bold blocks of color with the **1. Half-Moon Rising Hobo Bag** (page 8). Play with fabric strips and stitch accents in the quick-to-make **2. Odekake Tote** (page 14). Combine textures and curved piecing in the **3. Corduroy Patchwork Bag** (page 24) for the perfect fall purse. Take a trip back to the 1980s with an updated **4. Patchwork Bermuda Bag** (page 18) featuring simple graphic prints. Experiment with tone-on-tone colors and prints in the roomy **5. Checkerboard Bag** (page 28). Let the fabric be your guide, and you can never go wrong!

half-moon rising
HOBO BAG

A tiled-floor design inspired the patchwork for this generously sized hobo bag. Improvisational piecing joins half-moon fabric shapes in a fearless mix of colors, patterns, and prints. To achieve the signature, slouchy style of a hobo, the exterior and lining are gathered along the top of the bag, and a short strip of wide webbing creates the strap. The result is a practical, roomy bag that is bursting with color. *by* **MALKA DUBRAWSKY**

FABRIC

— Sixteen assorted 6" × 6" (15 cm × 15 cm) warm-colored cotton fabric pieces (*shown:* red and orange)

— Sixteen assorted 6" × 6" (15 cm × 15 cm) cool-colored cotton fabric pieces (*shown:* blue and green)

— ⅜ yd (34.5 cm) each of two 45" (114.5 cm) wide neutral cotton solids for block backgrounds (*shown:* dark gray and light gray)

— ⅜ yd (34.5 cm) of 45" (114.5 cm) wide coordinating cotton fabric for side and bottom panels

— 1⅜ yd (125.5 cm) of 45" (114.5 cm) wide cotton fabric for lining

— 1⅜ yd (125.5 cm) of 45" (114.5 cm) wide muslin

OTHER SUPPLIES

— Cardboard or template plastic

— Coordinating cotton sewing thread

— 1¼ yd (114.5 cm) of ½" (1.3 cm) wide double-fold bias tape

— 20" (51 cm) of 1½" (3.8 cm) wide cotton webbing for handle

— 1¼" (3.2 cm) wide button

— Rotary cutter, rigid acrylic ruler, and self-healing mat

— Handsewing needle

— Templates on pattern insert

— *Optional:* Quilt basting pins

FINISHED SIZE

— 20" × 20" × 3" (51 × 51 × 7.5 cm), excluding strap

NOTES

— All seam allowances are ¼" (6 mm) unless otherwise noted.

— Press seams to one side, alternating sides where seams intersect.

CUT THE FABRIC

1 Cut the following pieces as directed. To make templates, trace Pattern A and Pattern B (see pattern insert) onto cardboard or template plastic; cut out.

From assorted warm-colored pieces:

—Sixteen half-moon shapes (piece A) using template A

From assorted cool-colored pieces:

—Sixteen half-moon shapes (piece A) using template A

From first neutral-colored solid:

—Sixteen backgrounds (piece B) using template B

From second neutral-colored solid:

—Sixteen backgrounds (piece B) using template B

From the fabric for the side and bottom panels:

—Four 2" × 22" (5 × 56 cm) side strips

—Two 2" × 25" (5 × 63.5 cm) bottom strips

From the lining fabric:

—Two 23" × 22" (58.5 × 56 cm) rectangles

From the muslin:

—Two 24" × 24" (61 × 61 cm) squares

MAKE THE PATCHWORK

2 Fold one half-moon piece (A) and one background piece (B) in half and crease (**figure 1**); unfold.

3 With right sides facing, pin A to B along the curved edge, matching the creased centers and raw edges (**figure 2**). Sew together, easing the curved edges. Press seam to one side, clipping the seam allowance if necessary.

4 Repeat Steps 2 and 3 to make a total of thirty-two patchwork squares. (*Note:* Combine all warm-colored A pieces with one neutral solid and all cool-colored A pieces with the second neutral solid or mix as desired.)

5 Pin two warm-colored patchwork squares, right sides together, to make a half-moon shape. Sew the squares together with a ¼" (6 mm) seam allowance (**figure 3**). Press seam allowance to one side. Repeat to make a total of eight warm-colored block pairs.

6 With right sides together, pin and sew two pairs together so that the curved sides of half-moons meet in the center. Repeat to make a total of four warm-colored blocks (**figure 4**).

7 Repeat Steps 5 and 6 with the cool-colored patchwork squares to create a total of four cool-colored blocks.

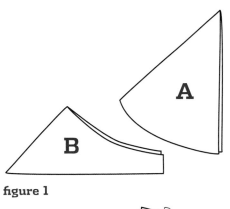

figure 1

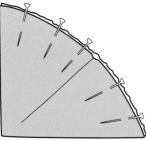

figure 2

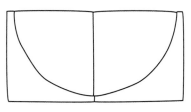

figure 3

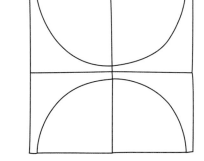

figure 4

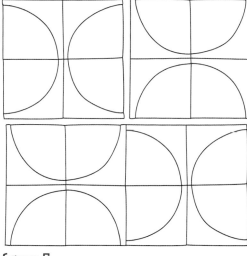

figure 5

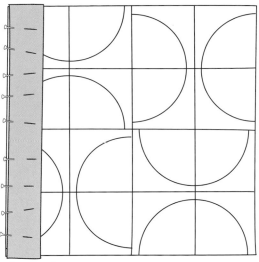

figure 6

8 With right sides together, pin and sew one cool-colored block and one warm-colored block together with a ¼" (6 mm) seam allowance (**figure 5**). Press seam open. Repeat to sew a second pair of blocks.

9 With right sides together, pin and sew these pairs together to complete bag side; press seam open.

10 Repeat Steps 8 and 9 to complete the second bag side.

11 Working on a flat surface, place one bag side, patch-work side up, on top of one muslin square; pin or baste the layers together. Free-motion quilt the patchwork side and then trim to finish first patchwork panel. Repeat to complete the second patchwork panel.

ASSEMBLE THE BAG

12 Pin one 2" × 22" (5 × 56 cm) strip to the side of one patchwork panel, right sides together (**figure 6**).

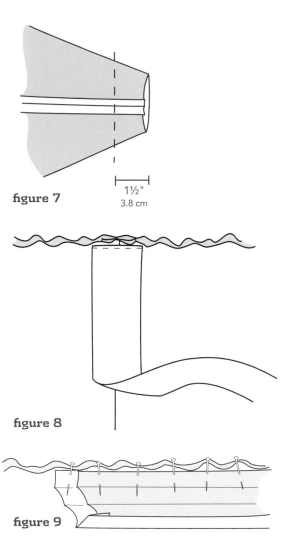

figure 7

1½"
3.8 cm

figure 8

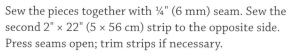

figure 9

Sew the pieces together with ¼" (6 mm) seam. Sew the second 2" × 22" (5 × 56 cm) strip to the opposite side. Press seams open; trim strips if necessary.

13 With right sides together, pin and sew one 2" × 25" (5 × 63.5 cm) strip to the bottom of the patchwork panel. Press the seam open; trim strip if necessary.

14 Repeat Steps 12 and 13 add strips to the second patchwork panel.

15 With right sides together, pin and sew the side and bottom edges of the patchwork panels together. Press seams open.

16 To create a flat base for bag bottom, match right sides and center seams of side and bottom; fold out a triangle with a height of 1½" (3.8 cm). Sew along base (**figure 7**). Repeat for the opposite edge of bag bottom.

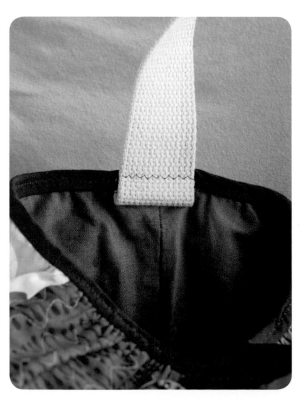

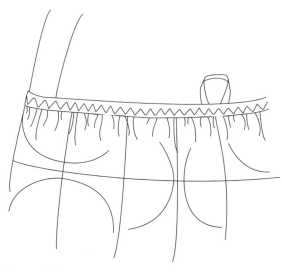

figure 10

17 Pin the 23" × 22" (58.5 × 56 cm) lining fabric rectangles with right sides together; sew along sides and bottom. Press the seams open.

18 Repeat Step 16 to create a flat base for lining bottom.

19 With wrong sides together, insert the lining inside patchwork bag. Pin the patchwork bag exterior and lining along the top edge, matching the side seams. Run a basting stitch through both layers ¼" (6 mm) from top raw edge.

20 Gather the top edge of the bag so that the opening measures approximately 16½" (42 cm). Machine baste the gathering in place with a ¼" (6 mm) seam.

21 Cut a 6" (15 cm) length of double-fold bias tape for the button loop. Sew two rows of topstitching ⅛" (3 mm) from both long folded edges.

22 Pin the short raw ends of the button loop to the raw gathered edge of the bag opening at the center of one side, making sure the button loop points toward the bag interior. Machine baste the button loop ¼" (6 mm) from the edge. *Note: This point now indicates back of bag.*

23 Pin the raw edges of the webbing strap to the lining, centering one end on each lining side seam along the top edge; machine baste in place (**figure 8**).

24 Cut the double-fold bias tape 33½" (85 cm) long. Open up one fold and pin tape along the raw top edge with the right sides facing (**figure 9**). Fold the short edge of the bottom bias tape end under before sewing to finish edge. Stitch inside the crease of the tape to attach it to the bag, catching the button loop and strap ends in the stitching.

25 Wrap the double-fold bias tape over the top of the raw edge of the bag and pin in place, flipping the button loop and the strap ends straight up. Using a zigzag stitch, stitch the tape in place, catching the strap ends and the button loop in the stitching (**figure 10**).

26 Sew the button in place.

Odekake is a Japanese word for going for a little walk, and this easy and quick-to-make quilted tote is perfect for touring around town. It's also a great way to use your favorite fabric scraps in clever, unevenly arranged appliqués. *by* **AYUMI TAKAHASHI**

odekake TOTE

FABRIC
— ½ yd (46 cm) of 45" (114.5 cm) wide Kona cotton for shell top (Main)
— ¼ yd (23 cm) of natural linen for shell base (Contrast A)
— ½ yd (46 cm) of 45" (114.5 cm) wide print cotton for lining (Contrast B)
— ⅛ yd (11.5 cm) of denim or recycled adult-size jeans for shell handles (Contrast C)
— ⅛ yd (11.5 cm) of 45" (114.5 cm) wide print cotton for lining handles (Contrast D)
— Eight different fabric scraps (cotton and/or linen prints work great; at least 1¼" × 10"–14" (3.2 × 25.5–35.5 cm))

OTHER SUPPLIES
— ½ yd (46 cm) of low-loft cotton batting
— ½ yd (46 cm) of fusible web
— Cotton sewing thread to contrast with top
— Cotton sewing thread to match lining handles
— Cotton sewing thread to contrast with fabric scraps
— Embroidery thread to contrast with shell base
— Quilting spray adhesive
— 5" (12.5 cm) of ⅛ " (3 mm) wide ribbon
— Hand embroidery needle
— Clear acrylic ruler
— Fabric marking pen

FINISHED SIZE
— About 13½" long × 11½" wide (34.5 × 29 cm) without handles. With handles, the bag is about 22" (56 cm) in height.

NOTE
— All seam allowances are ¼" (6 mm) unless otherwise noted.

CUT THE FABRIC

1 Cut the following pieces as directed:

From Main fabric cut:
—Two 11" × 12½" (28 × 31.5 cm) pieces for shell top.

From Contrast A fabric cut:
—Two 4" × 12½" (10 × 31.5 cm) pieces for shell base.

From Contrast B fabric cut:
—Two 14½" × 12½" (37 × 31.5 cm) pieces for lining.

From Contrast C fabric cut:
—Two 2¼" × 19" (5.5 × 48.5 cm) pieces for shell handles.

From Contrast D fabric cut:
—Two 2¼" × 19" (5.5 × 48.5 cm) pieces for lining handles.

From batting cut:
—Two 15½" × 13½" (39.5 × 34.5 cm) pieces.

APPLIQUÉ FABRIC SCRAPS

2 Following the manufacturer's instructions, iron the fusible web onto the wrong sides of the eight fabric scraps.

3 Cut out two 1¼" (3.2 cm) wide strips from each of the fabric scraps, ranging in length from 5" to 6½" (12.5 to 16.5 cm).

4 Place the two Shell Top pieces, right side up, in front of you, with the shorter (11" [28 cm]) edges at the top and bottom.

5 Peel the paper backing off eight of the fabric strips (one of each type/print). You will be arranging the strips along the left edge of one of the Shell Top pieces; start about 1" to 1¼" (2.5 to 3.2 cm) above the bottom edge and align one short edge of each strip with the raw edge of the Shell Top piece, placing the strips one after another and overlapping them slightly (see photo opposite). Following the manufacturer's instructions, iron the strips in place.

6 Using contrasting thread, topstitch around three edges of each strip (leaving the outer short edge unstitched), stitching very close to the edges. Sewing several haphazard lines of stitching will give a fun, handmade look; use the contrasting color thread or try using a few different colors of thread to add visual interest.

7 Repeat Steps 5 and 6 to appliqué the remaining eight strips along the left edge of the other shell top piece. (This will give you the look of the bag shown here, with the strips on opposite edges of the finished bag. If you would prefer to have them on the same side so that they seem to wrap around the bag, appliqué this set of strips to the right side of the second Shell Top instead.)

ASSEMBLE THE SHELL

8 Place one Shell Top piece right sides together with one Shell Base piece, aligning the 12½" (31.5 cm) edges at the bottom of the top piece; pin together. Sew together along the pinned edge (be sure to remove pins as you go!). Repeat with the remaining Shell Top and Shell Bases pieces. You now have two completed shell pieces, each measuring 14½" × 12½" (37 × 31.5 cm).

9 Place the two completed shell pieces in front of you, right side down, on a surface protected by newspaper or plastic bags. Following the manufacturer's instructions, use quilting spray adhesive to baste (see Stitch Glossary, page 126) one of the 15½" × 13½" (39.5 × 34.5 cm) pieces of batting, centered, to the wrong side of one of the shell pieces (1" [2.5 cm] of the batting will hang past the shell piece on each edge). Repeat to baste together the remaining batting and shell pieces.

10 Turn the shell pieces over so that the right sides are facing up. *Use the ruler and a fabric marking pen to draw a horizontal line across one shell piece, ⅜" (1 cm) from the top edge. Repeat to draw horizontal lines every ⅜" (1 cm) down the top shell piece only (do not draw lines on the shell base). With contrasting thread, machine quilt the shell, using a straight stitch and stitching over the drawn lines. Repeat from * to quilt the remaining shell piece.

11 Using contrasting embroidery thread, handstitch a line of running stitches on one Shell Base, about 1/16" (2 mm) below the seam between the Shell Top and the

✚ Always use high-quality interfacing. It might cost a little more, but will be easier to handle and less likely to bubble when fused. Buy it in bulk instead of in a package so you can feel its weight and drape (and save a little money too).
—AYUMI TAKAHASHI

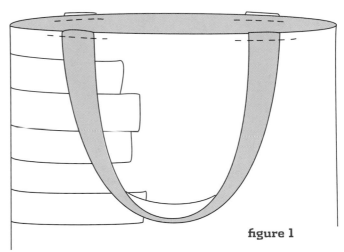

figure 1

Shell Base. Repeat the entire step on the remaining shell piece.

12 Fold the ribbon in half widthwise, wrong sides together. Align the short edges of the ribbon with the raw edge at the right side of one shell piece, 1½" (3.8 cm) above the bottom edge, and pin (the ribbon will lie on top of the shell base). Machine baste across the edges of the ribbon, about ⅛" (3 mm) from the raw edge, to secure the ribbon in place.

13 Place the two shell pieces right sides together, aligning all edges and making sure the ribbon loop is sandwiched in between; pin together around the edges. Sew together along the side and bottom edges, leaving the top open. Clip the bottom corners and turn the shell right side out.

MAKE THE HANDLES

14 Place one Shell Handle right sides together with one Lining Handle, aligning all edges. Pin and then sew together at one long (19" [48.5 cm]) edge. Open out the seamed handle pieces and then fold each long raw edge toward the wrong side so that the raw edges meet at the seam; press. Refold the handle along the seam, wrong sides together, and pin along the open long edge. You now have a handle that is 1" (2.5 cm) wide.

15 Using matching thread, topstitch along each long edge of the handle, ⅛" (3 mm) from the edge (this will also close the open edge).

16 Repeat Steps 14 and 15 with the remaining Shell and Lining Handle pieces.

SEW THE LINING

17 Place the two lining pieces right sides together and pin. Sew together at both long edges and one short edge, leaving a 4" (10 cm) gap in the short (bottom) edge. Leave the other short edge open for the bag top.

18 Clip the bottom corners.

FINISH THE TOTE

19 Measure 2½" (6.5 cm) from each side edge of the shell bag and mark on the front and back raw edges. Place one handle on each side of the shell bag, right sides together, aligning the short edges of the handle with the top raw edge of the shell bag at the marks (the outer edge of the handle ends should be at the marks). Machine baste the handle ends in place, ⅛" (3 mm) from the edge (**figure 1**).

20 With the lining still inside out, pull it up around the shell, aligning the side seams and the top edges. Make sure the handles are sandwiched in between; pin and then stitch together around the top edge. Carefully pull the shell through the opening in the bottom of the lining. Turn in the seam allowances at the opening and finger press, then handstitch closed with a slip stitch. Stuff the lining down inside the shell.

21 Topstitch around the top edge of the bag, ⅛" (3 mm) from the edge.

The Bermuda bag—a casual bag with wooden handles and an oval shape—was a popular accessory in the 1980s. For an updated look, designer Blair Stocker created graphic patchwork fabric panels (made easy with fusible interfacing), and spray-painted wooden handles in a fashion-forward color for the perfect summer carryall. *by* **BLAIR STOCKER**

patchwork
BERMUDA BAG

FABRIC
—At least nine different fat quarters of cotton prints (*Note:* two charm packs of at least thirty 5" (12.5 cm) squares would also work.)

—½ yd (45.5 cm) of 45" (114.5 cm) wide coordinating cotton fabric for lining

—Two 22" × 22" (56 × 56 cm) pieces of muslin

OTHER SUPPLIES
—Two 22" × 22" (56 × 56 cm) pieces of low loft batting

—Two 20" × 20" (51 × 51 cm) pieces of fusible featherweight interfacing

—Coordinating cotton sewing thread

—One pair of natural wooden handles 9¾" (25 cm) wide

—One piece of fine grit sandpaper

—Spray paint for bag handles

—Black fine-line marker

—Handsewing needle

—Bermuda Bag template on pattern insert

—Rotary cutter, rigid acrylic ruler, and self-healing mat

—Handsewing needle

—Fabric marking pen

—*Optional:* blue painter's tape

—*Optional:* zipper foot for sewing machine

FINISHED SIZE
10½" × 14" (26.5 × 35.5 cm) including handles

NOTES
—When choosing fabrics for the patchwork, try a mix of small and large prints. Fussy-cut designs out of larger prints to create several different patchwork squares from a single fabric.

—A fat quarter measures 18" × 22" (45.5 × 56 cm). Charm squares are sold in collections or packs and each square measures 5" (12.5 cm)

—Sand, wipe away dust, and then paint both sides of the wooden handles before constructing the bag. Apply several light coats, allowing drying time between coats as directed by manufacturer.

Allow the handles to dry for twenty-four hours before the final assembly. Spray paint in a well-ventilated area, on a protected work surface, wearing protective gloves and a mask.

CREATE PATCHWORK PANELS

1 Using a ruler and a black fine-line marker, draw a grid of 2½" (6.5 cm) squares on the adhesive side of one piece of interfacing, eight rows across and eight rows down for a 64-square grid (lines should also be visible on the non-adhesive side). Repeat with the remaining piece of interfacing. Trim away any extra interfacing.

2 Cut a total of 128 2½" (6.5 cm) squares from fat quarter prints. Arrange the squares right side up on the interfacing grid. When the grid is covered, press the entire piece carefully according to the manufacturer's instructions. Repeat with the second piece of interfacing.

3 To sew a patchwork panel, fold the panel with right sides together on one vertical line of the interfacing grid. Sew a ¼" (6 mm) seam all the way down that line (**figure 1**). Repeat this with all the vertical grid lines. Clip the seam allowances open at the gridline cross points and press the seams open (**figure 2a**). Repeat with the horizontal gridlines. Repeat this step with the second patchwork panel. The sewn patchwork panels should each measure 16½" × 16½" (42 × 42 cm) (**figure 2**).

4 Layer one piece of muslin, one piece of batting, and one patchwork panel, right side up; pin or baste the layers together.

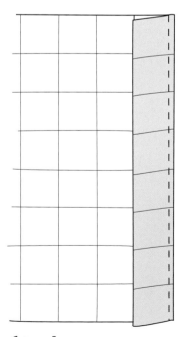

figure 1

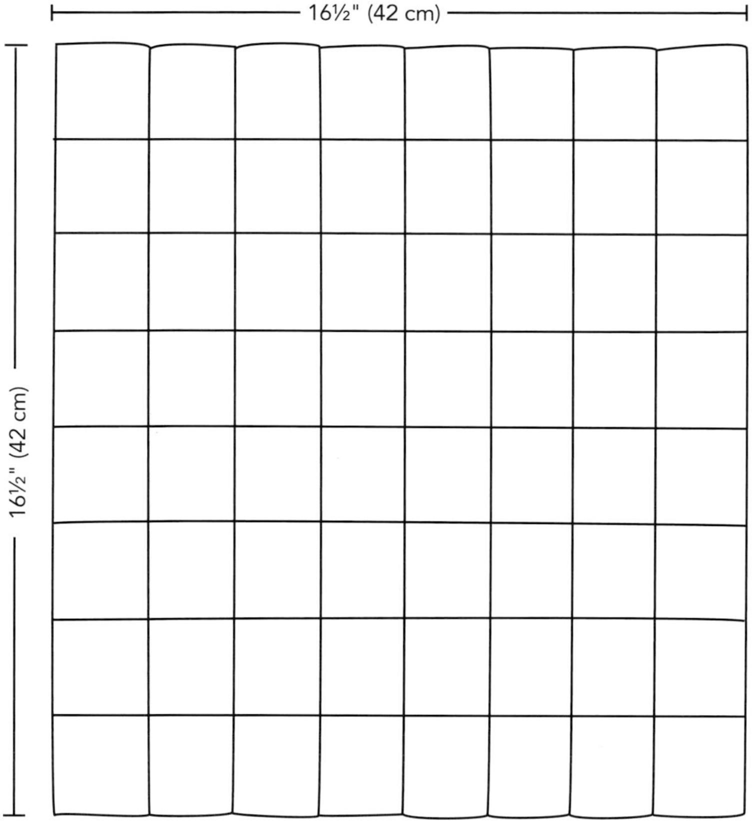

├─────── 16½" (42 cm) ───────┤

(grid figure with left measurement 16½" (42 cm))

figure 2

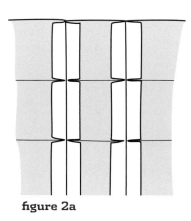

figure 2a

5 To quilt, use either a fabric marking pen or blue painter's tape to mark a diagonal line through the corners of each square. Begin in the center and work toward each edge in both diagonal directions. Machine quilt through all layers.

6 Repeat Steps 4 and 5 with the second patchwork panel.

CONSTRUCT THE BAG

7 Using the Bermuda Bag pattern on Pattern Insert, cut a bag piece from each of the quilted patchwork panels (**figure 3**). Cut two pieces from the lining fabric.

8 Using a fabric marking pen, measure 3" (7.5 cm) from the top of each of the patchwork panels and place a mark on the wrong side on each side edge. Do the

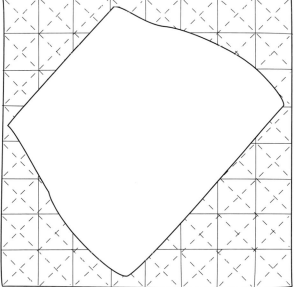

figure 3

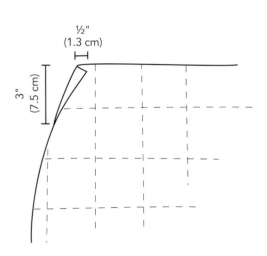

figure 4

figure 5

same for the lining panels. Turn back a ½" (1.3 cm) hem at the top corners, angled to and stopping at the side marks (**figure 4**).

9 With right sides together, sew one of the patchwork panels to one of the lining pieces across the top with a ¼" (6 mm) seam allowance. Press the seam allowance open. Repeat with the remaining patchwork panel and lining piece.

10 Pull one of the lining/patchwork pairs through the opening of one of the wooden handles, right side facing out (**figure 5**). Sew a line of stitching through all layers 1" (2.5 cm) below the handle. (*Note:* A zipper foot is helpful.) Repeat with the remaining handle and lining/patchwork pair.

11 Place the lining pieces right sides together and pin. Put the patchwork bag panels right sides together and pin (the wooden handles are now in the middle). Leaving a 6" (15 cm) opening at the bottom of the lining panels for turning, sew the sides using a ¼" (6 mm) seam allowance and stopping at the marks made on the side in Step 8 (**figure 6**).

12 Turn the bag right side out by pulling it through the opening in the lining; press. Turn the opening of the lining towards the inside; handstitch the opening closed.

13 Topstitch the side openings as shown in **figure 7**.

RESOURCES

Blair recommends the following brands:

"Echo" by Lotta Jansdotter for Windham Fabrics (windhamfabrics.net)

Sunbelt Fastener natural wood handles (sunbeltfastener.com)

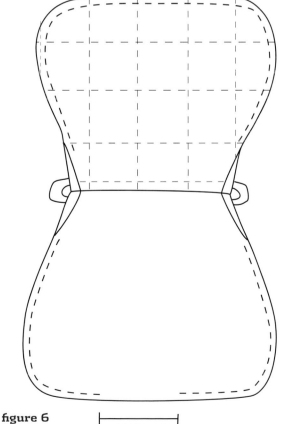

figure 6

6" (15 cm)

figure 7

This cute patchwork handbag is the ideal project for using up fabric scraps and highlighting some of your favorite prints. Perfect for fall, it has a simple button closure and a pretty print lining to safely hold your essentials.

by **REBEKA LAMBERT**

corduroy patchwork HANDBAG

FABRIC

—½ yd (45.5 cm) of 45" (114.5 cm) wide corduroy (Main)

—⅜ yd (34 cm) of 45" (114.5 cm) wide cotton print for lining (Contrast A)

—6½" × 8" (16.5 × 20.5 cm) of cotton print (Contrast B)

—8½" × 8" (21.5 × 20.5 cm) of cotton print (Contrast C)

—4½" × 4½" (11.5 × 11.5 cm) of cotton print (Contrast D)

OTHER SUPPLIES

—⅜ yd (34 cm) of 45" (114.5 cm) wide fusible fleece

—Sewing thread to match corduroy

—One 1⅛" (28 mm) diameter button

—Corduroy Patchwork Bag pattern templates on Pattern Insert

FINISHED SIZE

6½" tall × 10½" wide × 3½" deep (16.5 × 26.5 × 9 cm).

NOTES

—The seam allowance for piecing the purse front is ¼" (6 mm); all other seam allowances are ⅜" (1 cm) unless otherwise noted.

—For best results when piecing the purse front, begin by lining up the outer edges, and then work toward the center.

—When cutting the patchwork pieces, pin the pattern, right side up, to the fabric right side. When a reversed piece is called for, pin the pattern, wrong side up, to the fabric right side, creating a mirror image of the piece.

CUT THE FABRIC

1 Trace the pattern templates from the Pattern Insert. Cut the following pieces as directed; label the pieces on the wrong side for easier identification, especially the A and D pieces, which are very similar in shape and size:

From Main Fabric:

—One Purse Body on fold

—One each of A, B, and D

—One each of A reversed and C reversed

—Two 4 × 18" (10 × 45.5 cm) rectangles for straps with the corduroy wales parallel to the short ends

—One 1½ × 6½" (3.8 × 16.5 cm) rectangle for loop closure with the corduroy wales parallel to the short ends

From Contrast A:

—Two Purse Bodies on fold for lining

From Contrast B:

—One B reversed

From Contrast C:

—One C

From Contrast D:

—One D reversed

From the Fusible Fleece:

—Two Purse Bodies on fold

PREPARE THE PURSE FRONT

Note: Refer to the diagram at right for assistance with the following steps.

2 Piece the front of the purse in two halves. Lay the four pieces labeled A, B, C, and D on the work surface as they will be arranged in the finished purse. *Pin pieces A and B, right sides together, from the side edge to the center front. Stitch with a ¼" (6 mm) seam. Press the seam open, clipping if necessary to release the fabric so the seam allowances will lie flat. Topstitch ⅛" (3 mm) from the seam on either side, sewing through the fabric and seam allowances. Repeat from * to join pieces C and D, then stitch the two units together to complete one half of the purse front.

3 Repeat Step 2 to join the reversed A, B, C, and D pieces to assemble the other half of the purse front. With right sides together, matching the seams, sew the two halves together at the center front with a ¼" (6 mm) seam to complete the purse front. Press the seam open.

Following the manufacturer's instructions, fuse the fleece to the wrong side of the assembled purse front and the Main fabric Purse Body (this is the purse back). Repeat from * to join pieces C and D, then stitch the two units together to complete one half of the purse front.

ASSEMBLE THE PURSE BODY

Note: Beginning here, use ⅜" (1 cm) seam allowances, unless otherwise noted.

4 With right sides together, sew the purse front and back together along the sides and bottom. Press the seams toward the purse back.

5 With right sides together, sew the purse lining (Contrast A Purse Body pieces) along the sides and bottom, leaving a 4" to 5" (10 to 12.5 cm) gap at the center of the bottom seam. Press the seams toward the purse front.

✚ Always trim seam allowances and clip curves, even though these steps are not visible on the outside of the finished bag. Careful trimming and clipping make sewing through bulky seams while assembling the bag easier, and give the bag a smoother finished look. —REBEKA LAMBERT

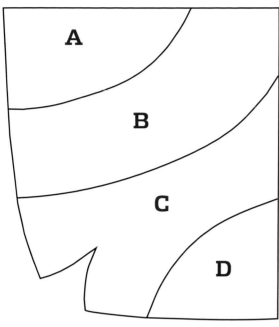

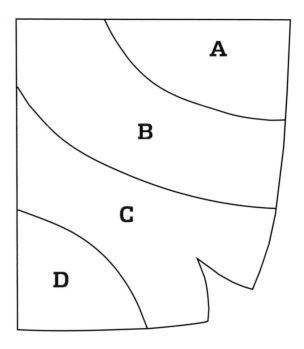

diagram

SEW THE BOTTOM CORNERS

6 Fold the purse, right sides together, so one side seam is aligned with the bottom seam. The open edges at the corner will align, forming a curved edge. Sew along the curve to box the purse corner. Repeat to box the other purse corner, and then repeat again to box both corners of the purse lining.

MAKE THE STRAPS AND LOOP

7 Press each strap in half, lengthwise, wrong sides together. Open the fold and bring each long raw edge to meet the center crease; press. Refold each strap along its central crease, enclosing the raw edges. Edgestitch ⅛" (3 mm) from both long edges of each strap. Repeat entire step to prepare the loop closure.

8 Pin the ends of one strap to the purse front, right sides together, with each strap end 3" (7.5 cm) from the nearest side seam, matching the raw edges. Make sure the strap is not twisted. Repeat to pin the second strap to the purse back.

9 Pin both ends of the loop closure to the right side of the purse back at the center, matching the raw edges. Make sure the loop is not twisted.

JOIN PURSE AND LINING

10 Insert the purse, right side out, into the lining, wrong side out, so the right sides are together, with the straps and loop closure sandwiched between the purse and lining. Align the raw edges of the lining and purse, matching the side seams. Sew the lining to the purse along the upper edge.

11 Reaching through the gap in the lining bottom seam, pull the corduroy shell through the lining to turn the purse right side out.

FINISH THE BAG

12 Press the lining into place along the top of the purse, and then topstitch ¼" (6 mm) from the upper edge.

13 Turn in the seam allowances at the gap in the lining seam and then close gap by machine or handsew closed with a slip stitch.

14 Sew the button to the purse center front, 1¼" (3.2 cm) below the upper edge, and fasten the loop around the button.

Mix several shades of linen to create this quilted patchwork bag inspired by wooden checkerboards. Its roomy design, soft flannel lining, and inside pocket will ensure it carries everything you need. Machine embroidery accents the patchwork and fabric handles. *by* **AYUMI TAKAHASHI**

checkerboard BAG

FABRIC
—½ yd (45.5 cm) each of two different colors of 45" (114.5 cm) wide linen for patchwork and handles (A and B; *shown:* two different shades of natural linen)

—½ yd (45.5 cm) each of two different colors of 45" (114.5 cm) wide linen for patchwork, circle appliqué, and shell base (C and D; *shown:* two different shades of dark brown)

—¼ yd (23 cm) each of 2 different 45" (114.5 cm) wide linen prints for circle appliqué (E and F; *shown:* two different natural linen prints)

—8" (20.5 cm) square scrap of linen plaid for circle appliqué (G; *shown:* natural linen plaid)

—⅛ yd (11.5 cm) of 45" (114.5 cm) wide print cotton for lining handles (H; *shown:* brown polka dot)

—¾ yd (68.5 cm) of 45" (114.5 cm) wide flannel for lining (I; *shown:* tan)

—5½" × 10½" (14 × 26.5 cm) piece of print cotton for pocket (J; *shown:* white polka dot)

OTHER SUPPLIES
—¾ yd (68.5 cm) of cotton batting (Recommended: Warm and Natural cotton batting)

—1 yd (91.5 cm) of paper-backed fusible web

—5" (12.5 cm) square of lightweight fusible interfacing

—Cotton sewing thread to match fabrics A/B

—Cotton sewing thread to match fabrics C/D

—Cotton sewing thread to match flannel

—2" (5 cm) of ⅝" (1.5 cm) wide ribbon (optional)

—Handsewing needle

—Quilt-basting spray

—Fabric marking pencil

—Walking foot and quilting guide (optional) for sewing machine

—Templates on pattern insert

FINISHED SIZE
About 15" high without handles × 20" wide at the top (38 × 51 cm); 12" (30.5 cm) wide at the bottom

NOTES
—All seam allowances are ¼" (6 mm) unless otherwise noted.

CUT THE FABRIC

1 Cut the following pieces as directed; you may want to label pieces on the wrong side with a fabric pencil or use tape for temporary labels to avoid confusion as you put the bag together.

From fabric A:

—Sixteen 3½" (9 cm) squares for patchwork

—Two 2¼" × 25" (5.5 × 63.5 cm) strips for Shell Handles

From fabric B:

—Nineteen 3½" (9 cm) squares for patchwork

From fabric C:

—Fifteen 3½" (9 cm) squares for patchwork

—One 7" × 14" (18 × 35.5 cm) piece for Shell Base

—Eighteen 3" (7.5 cm) squares for Circle Appliqués

From fabric D:

—Twenty 3½" (9 cm) squares for patchwork

—Seventeen 3" (7.5 cm) squares for Circle Appliqués

From fabric E:

—Nine 3" (7.5 cm) squares for Circle Appliqués

From fabric F:

—Ten 3" (7.5 cm) squares for Circle Appliqués

From fabric G:

—Six Circle Appliqués (following method described in Step 6)

From fabric H:

—Two 2¼" × 25" (5.5 × 63.5 cm) strips for Lining Handles

From fabric I:

—Two 20¾" × 15¼" (52.5 × 39.5 cm) pieces for Lining

—One Lining Base using Shell/Lining Base pattern

From the cotton batting:

—Two 25½" × 19½" (65 × 49.5 cm) pieces for Shell Interlining

—Two 11" × 18" (28 × 45.5 cm) pieces for Shell Base Interlining

ASSEMBLE THE SHELL

2 Using the linen 3½" (9 cm) squares (fabrics A, B, C, and D), create two 7 × 5 patchwork panels in a checkered pattern. Begin by placing a light and a dark linen square right sides together and seaming along one side. Add five more patches, alternating dark and

light squares, to make a seven-patch row. Repeat to make nine more seven-patch rows, then join the rows to make two panels of five rows each.

3 Spray the wrong side of each patchwork panel with quilt-basting spray and center it right side up on one of the Shell Interlining batting pieces.

4 Machine quilt each panel by sewing a square about 1/16" (2 mm) inside the patchwork seams on each of the square patches, using thread that matches the patch and a walking foot if desired. Along the outer edges of the patchwork, the quilted squares should be about 5/16" (8 mm) from the raw edges so they aren't obscured by seams sewn later.

5 Using the provided Circle Appliqué template, draw 60 circles on the paper side of the fusible web, leaving 1" (2.5 cm) between circles.

6 Rough cut these circles, leaving a small extra margin of fusible web around each, then fuse one to the wrong side of each 3" (7.5 cm) square (cut from fabrics C, D, E, and F). Cut out the circles along the drawn lines on the fusible web, peel off the paper backing, and fuse each circle onto a square patch in the patchwork panels, placing light-colored circles on dark square patches and dark circles on light squares. (There will be five patches without a circle on each side of the bag, so arrange your circles as desired or refer to the photo on page 28 for the arrangement seen in the sample.) This will now be referred to as the shell.

7 To secure the Circle Appliqués of fabrics C, D, E, F, and G to the shell, machine quilt around each Circle Appliqué using a zigzag stitch about 1/16"–1/8" (2–3 mm) wide and 1 mm long (25 stitches per inch) with thread that matches the square patch under the circle, pivoting frequently with the needle in the square patch.

+ Make a freezer-paper template whenever a pattern calls for anything other than a simple square or rectangle shape. This saves time and ensures the accuracy of shapes cut from fabric. —AYUMI TAKAHASHI

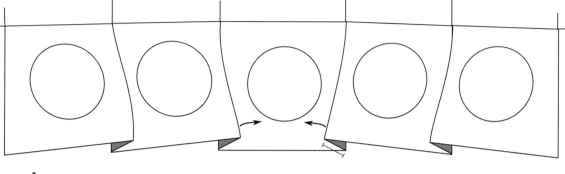

figure 1

8 Place the patchwork panels right sides together (making sure the checkerboard pattern of the patchwork continues where the panels meet), pin, and sew the two short edges to make a tube. Set it aside.

9 Spray the wrong side of the fabric C Shell Base with quilt-basting spray and center it right side up on one of the Shell Base Interlining batting pieces. Spray the remaining Shell Base Interlining batting piece and adhere it to the other side of the first batting piece. Using matching thread and a walking foot, machine quilt in a diagonal grid pattern with lines spaced about ½" (1.3 cm) apart. Use the edge of your presser foot or a quilting guide to keep the spacing of the lines even.

10 Use the provided Shell/Lining Base pattern to cut the Shell Base from the quilted piece completed in Step 9 mark at the middle of each edge.

11 With right sides together, pin the Shell Base to the quilted shell from Step 8, aligning the notches on the curved ends of the Shell Base with the side seams of the shell and the notches on the straight edges of the Shell Base with the middle of each patchwork panel's bottom edge. Create ⅝" (1.5 cm) wide pleats to fit the shell to the Shell Base by folding the square patch seams toward the center of each side. Pin each pleat to secure, adjusting the depth of the pleats if necessary to fit the Shell Base (**figure 1**). Sew the shell and Shell Base together, being sure to catch the pleats in the stitching.

ASSEMBLE THE LINING

12 Fold the fabric J Pocket in half widthwise, with right sides together.

13 Sew the raw edges together, leaving a 2" (5 cm) opening in one edge for turning.

14 Fuse the 5" (12.5 cm) square of lightweight fusible interfacing to one side of the pocket. Turn the pocket right side out through the opening, folding in and finger- pressing the seam allowances at the opening.

15 Pin this pocket to the right side of one fabric I Lining piece, with the folded edge on top about 2¼" (5.5 cm) from the upper long edge of the Lining piece and the pocket centered between the short edges of the Lining. Fold the ribbon in half widthwise and

sandwich the raw ends between the pocket and the Lining at the right bottom edge (optional; see photo at right). Topstitch the sides and bottom edges of the pocket, reinforcing the ends of the stitching by sewing a small triangle of stitches near the top edge when starting and stopping.

16 Sew the two short edges of the two Lining pieces with right sides together to make a tube, leaving a 4½" (11.5 cm) opening at one side edge.

17 Pin the Lining Base to the lining tube with right sides together, aligning, pleating, and sewing as described in Step 11.

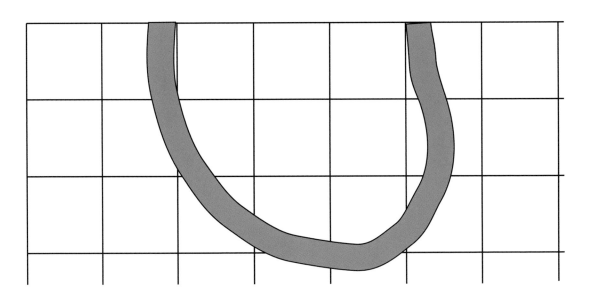

figure 2

MAKE THE HANDLES

18 Place one Shell Handle right sides together with one Lining Handle, aligning all edges. Pin and then sew together along one long (25" [63.5 cm]) edge. Open out the seamed handle pieces, press the seam allowances open, and then fold each long raw edge toward the wrong side so that the raw edges meet at the seams; press. Refold the handle along the seam, wrong sides together, and sew along the open long edge. Press flat. You now have a handle that is 1" (2.5 cm) wide. Repeat this entire step with the remaining Shell Handle and Lining Handle to make the second handle.

19 Using matching thread for both the top and the bobbin thread, topstitch along each long edge of the handles, ⅛" (3 mm) from the edge.

20 Using contrasting thread, straight stitch random zigzags from one long edge of each handle to the other long edge. Work from one end of the handle, zigzagging back and forth and pivoting with the needle in the fabric near the long edges, and when you reach the opposite end, turn the handle and zigzag randomly back over the handle again. Make several passes of zigzags this way to create the overlapped zigzag shown in the sample (see photo on page 28).

FINISHING

21 Place one handle on each side of the shell bag, right sides together, aligning the raw ends of the handle with the top raw edge of the shell bag and centering the handle with three square patches between the two handle ends (**figure 2**). Machine baste the handle ends in place, ⅛" (3 mm) from the edge.

22 With the Lining inside out, pull it up around the shell, aligning the side seams and the top raw edges. Make sure the handles are sandwiched in between; pin and then stitch together around the top edge. Carefully pull the shell through the opening in the side of the Lining. Turn in the seam allowances at the opening and finger press, then handstitch closed with a slip stitch. Stuff the Lining down inside the shell.

23 Topstitch around the top edge of the bag, ⅛" (3 mm) from the edge, being sure to keep the handles out of the way of the stitching.

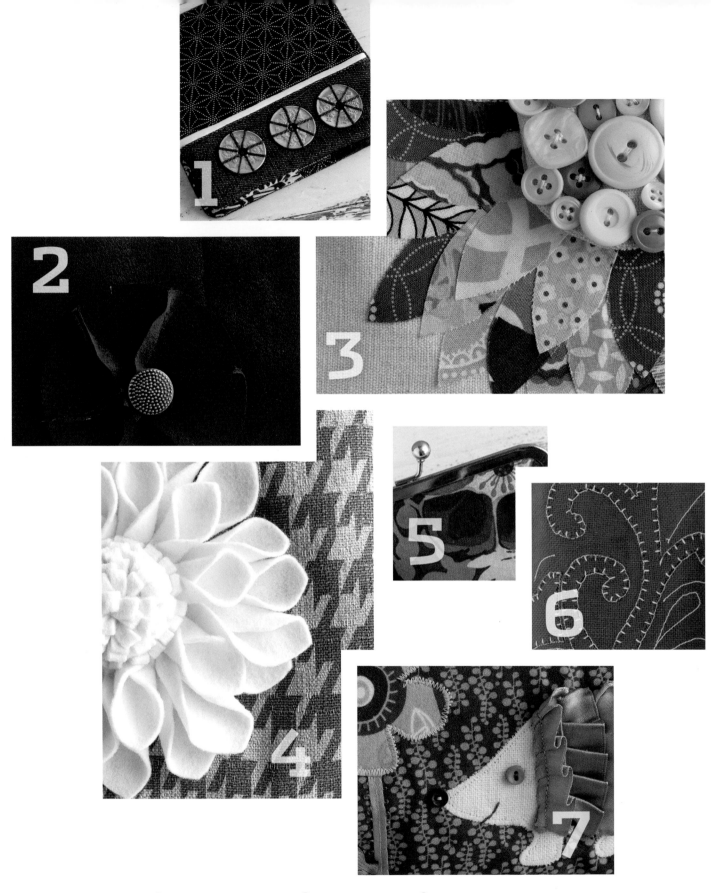

........*personalize your bag with unique accents*.....

creative embellishment

Whether you go big or go small, the right embellishment can turn a simple bag into a one-of-kind accessory. Appliqué, embroidery, and simple handstitching are fun and easy techniques to experiment with on all types of bags. Attach Japanese coins with handstitching for a unique accent on the **1. East Meets West Wallet** (page 48). Stitch stylish flowers to the fashionable suede **2. Dimensional Flower Handbag** (page 36). Showcase raw-edge applique in the **3. Pretty Petals Clutch** (page 58). Set off a fashionable winter wool bag with a stunning felt flower in the **4. Dahlia Purse** (page 52). Show off your hand-embroidery skills on the **5. Little Stitches Coin Purses** (page 42). Play with embroidery in the **6. Appliqué Linen Drawstring Bag** (page 62). Or use buttons, trim, and appliqué to make the super-cute **7. Zippy Pouches** (page 68). No matter which bag you choose to sew, make it your own!

dimensional flower HANDBAG

Accessorize in style with this chic faux-suede handbag featuring dimensional flower appliqués on the front pocket. The roomy, fully lined interior features a double pocket to keep your phone and keys handy. *by* **CAROL ZENTGRAF**

FABRIC
—¾ yd (68.5 cm) of 60" (152.5 cm) wide soft faux suede
—¾ yd (68.5 cm) of 45" (114.5 cm) wide coordinating cotton print fabric for lining

OTHER SUPPLIES
—2 yd (1.8 m) of 20" (51 cm) wide fusible interfacing
—Press cloth
—Matching sewing thread
—Handsewing needle
—Two 1" (2.5 cm) rectangular purse handle rings
—¾" (2 cm) magnetic handbag snap
—Five ½" (1.3 cm) round metal shank buttons
—Permanent fabric adhesive
—Self-adhesive, double-sided basting tape
—Tailor's chalk
—Dimensional Flower Handbag pattern and templates on Pattern Insert

FINISHED SIZE
—14" × 18" (35.5 × 45.5 cm) with 14" (35.5 cm) handle drop

NOTES
—All seam allowances are ½" (1.3 cm) unless otherwise noted. Sew seams with right sides together except where otherwise indicated.

—Finger press or use a pressing cloth and medium-low temperature to press the faux-suede. Do not touch the iron directly to it.

—Avoid using pins or ripping seams when working with suede, because holes may be permanent. Use self-adhesive, double-sided basting tape to secure layers when needed.

CUT AND PREPARE THE FABRIC

1 Trace the pattern and templates from the pattern insert, and cut out. Using tailor's chalk, transfer the pocket placement markings to one of the faux-suede handbag pieces.

Cut the following from the faux suede:

—Two Handbag pieces on the fold

—One Outer Pocket on the fold

—Eighteen Small Flower Petals

—Twelve Large Flower Petals

—One 2½" × 27" (6.5 × 68.5 cm) strip for the Handle

—Two 2½" × 3" (6.5 × 7.5 cm) strips for the Handle Loops

Cut the following from the cotton lining:

—Two Handbag pieces on the fold

—One Outer Pocket on the fold

—One 10½" × 12½" (26.5 × 31.5 cm) rectangle for the Interior Pocket

Cut the following from the fusible interfacing:

—Two Handbag pieces on the fold

—One 10½" × 12½" (26.5 × 31.5 cm) rectangle for the Interior Pocket

—One 2½" × 27" (6.5 × 68.5 cm) strip for the Handle

2 Using a press cloth, fuse the interfacing pieces to the wrong side of the corresponding suede pieces.

CREATE THE HANDBAG SHELL

3 To make each flower, sew the side edges of six petals together (sew the first and last petal together to complete the circular flower) with wrong sides to-

gether, using a ¼" (6 mm) seam allowance. Begin sewing from the outer edge and stitch toward the center, stopping ¼" (6 mm) from the tip. Use this technique to make three small and two large flowers.

4 Place the suede and lining fabric Outer Pockets right sides together. Sew, leaving a 3" (7.5 cm) opening in the bottom of the pocket for turning. Trim the seam allowances to ¼" (6 mm) and trim the corners, then turn the pocket right side out. Press the edges from the lining side, using a press cloth. Fold the seam allowances at the gap to the inside of the opening. Press so the seams lie flat and look neat. Close the opening with basting tape.

5 Arrange the flowers on the suede side of the Outer Pocket and glue the centers in place with permanent

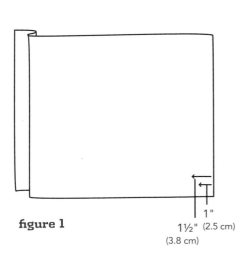

figure 1

1" 1½" (2.5 cm) (3.8 cm)

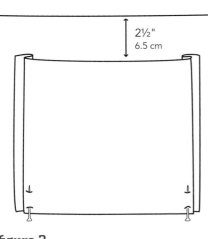

2½" 6.5 cm

figure 2

fabric adhesive. When the glue is dry, sew a button to the center of each flower, inserting the shank through the center of the flower. Make sure that your stitches penetrate only the suede, so that they do not show on the lining side of the pocket.

6 Center the Outer Pocket on one Handbag piece and secure the edges with basting tape. Edgestitch the pocket in place, leaving the top edge open and un-stitched. Stitch through the center of the pocket from the top to the bottom to create two pouches.

7 With right sides together, sew the darts located at the bottom of each Handbag piece. Sew the two Hand-bag pieces with right sides together, matching the darts and top edges and leaving the top edges open. Turn the shell right side out.

CREATE THE LINING

8 Fold the Interior Pocket rectangle in half length-wise and sew the side and bottom edges together, leaving an opening in the bottom edge for turning. Turn right side out and press, pressing the opening seam allowances under. Make a pleat at each corner to add fullness to the pocket by measuring and mark-ing 1" (2.5 cm) and 1½" (3.8 cm) from each corner on the bottom edge. Fold the pocket on one 1½" (3.8 cm) mark and bring the fold to meet the nearby 1" (2.5 cm) mark, forming a small pleat (**figure 1**). Pin the pleat at the bottom (stitched) edge to secure. Repeat to make a pleat near the second corner (refer to figure 1). Pin the pocket to the center of one Lining piece, 2½" (6.5 cm) from the top edge (**figure 2**, page

38). Edgestitch the side and bottom edges of the pock-et to the lining.

9 To add the magnetic snap to the lining, cut two 1" (2.5 cm) squares of fusible interfacing. On the wrong side of each lining piece, apply an interfacing square ¾" (2 cm) below the center of the top edge. Apply the snap halves to the right side of each lining piece ac-cording to the manufacturer's instructions, position-ing the top of the snap ⅜" (1 cm) from the top edge.

10 Sew the darts in the lining Handbag pieces. Sew the lining Handbag pieces right sides together, matching the darts and top edges. Leave the top edges open and leave a 4" (10 cm) opening in the center of the bottom edge.

INSERT THE LINING

11 Place the shell (suede) bag into the lining bag so that the right sides are together, matching the side seams and top edges. Sew the top edges together, leav-ing the handle openings unstitched. Trim the seam allowances to ¼" (6 mm) wide and clip the curves. Pull the shell bag through the opening in the lining to turn the lining right side out. Fold the seam allowances inside the opening, then press. Handsew the opening closed with a slip stitch. Insert the lining down into the bag.

MAKE THE HANDLES

12 To make the Handle and the Handle Loops, with the wrong sides of the strips facing up, turn the long edges of each strip under ¼" (6 mm) and adhere with basting tape. Fold each strip in half lengthwise with wrong sides together. Topstitch ⅛" (3 mm) from both long edges, making sure the basted edge stays in place.

13 Wrap 1" (2.5 cm) on each end of the handle around a handle ring. Topstitch across the handle, ½" (1.3 cm) from the fold. Stitch again ¼" (6 mm) from the first stitching. Wrap a handle loop around the opposite side of each handle ring with the short cut edges even and stitch across the handle loop ½" (1.3 cm) below the ring.

14 Turn under the seam allowances of each handle opening and secure with basting tape. Insert the raw edges of a handle loop into each opening, so that 1" (2.5 cm) is inside the bag. Topstitch the lining to the shell, ⅛" (3 mm) from the top edge of the handbag, while also stitching the handle loops in place. Back-tack over the portion that secures the handle loops for extra stability.

TIPS FOR SEWING WITH
ultrasuede

Ultrasuede is a polyester microfiber/polyurethane faux suede. The fabric is non-woven, so cut edges won't ravel. Looking very much like real suede, Ultrasuede is available in three weights: Ultrasuede Light, Ultrasuede Soft, and Ultrasuede Ambiance. Decorator weights are also available. Look for solids, embossed patterning, and animal prints. You'll find more than 100 colors as well as pattern combinations.

Unlike real leather, Ultrasuede breathes when you wear it, and it's resistant to damage by abrasion, so it tends to look new longer than its real suede cousins. It can be handwashed or machine-washed and machine dried—or dry-cleaned.

Most Ultrasuede is difficult to ease, so avoid patterns with close-fitting details. Changing seams in Ultrasuede isn't an option because needle holes show. In areas where interfacing is needed, opt for fusible and trim away all seam allowances before fusing it in place.

CUTTING
Because Ulstrasuede is nonwoven, pieces of Ultrasuede can be cut up to 45 degrees off grain, often saving fabric from the pattern layout diagram. Use a "with nap" layout to avoid shading. Pin only within the seam allowances because pin marks can be permanent, particularly in light-colored fabric. Use sharp scissors or a rotary cutter and cut a single layer if possible—the fabric is dense.

NEEDLE NOTES
Use a size 80/12 universal-point needle on Ultrasuede for the best stitching quality. If you have a problem with skipped stitches, try a Microtex (sharp) needle. When you use heavier thread for topstitching, choose a larger needle to accommodate the thread size. A double needle works well for topstitching Ultrasuede because it keeps stitch rows parallel.

SEAMING
Use 10 to 12 stitches per inch when seaming Ultrasuede and a slightly longer stitch for topstitching.

There are two Ultrasuede construction methods: conventional and flat. They can be used separately or together, depending on the project and the fabric weight.

To sew a conventional seam, place the pieces right sides together and place narrow basting tape between the layers within the seam allowance to prevent slippage (**figure 1**). Alternatively, you can use clips to hold the edges together. On Ultrasuede Light, hold the seam taut while stitching to avoid puckering.

Flat construction utilizes lapped seam lines. This method works well on heavier weights because seams are fused in place before stitching, and you don't need to worry about layers slipping as you sew.

To create a lapped seam, follow the general guideline that front laps back, as at shoulders and side seams. Trim away the seam allowance on the overlap section of the seam but leave the full seam allowance on the underlap.

Lap the seam allowance on the underlap to the trimmed overlap edge, placing a narrow strip of fusible web such as Steam-A-Seam2 ½" or ¼" tape between the layers. Using a press cloth to protect the fabric, fuse the layers together from the wrong side. Another option is to use basting tape to hold the layers together for stitching.

When you join garment sections, such as collars and facings, fuse the layers wrong sides together and trim off outer seam allowances through both layers.

PRESSING
Always use a press cloth between the iron and the Ultrasuede to avoid damaging the fabric surface. If you don't, there can be a permanent shine or iron imprint. A synthetic iron setting and steam work well.

It is best to press from the wrong side, but you should also use a napped cloth under the fabric right side to protect it. Press lightly; using the full weight of the iron can leave a seam allowance imprint on the fabric right side.

A conventional seam is usually pressed open after stitching, using a wooden clapper to help flatten the seam itself. For a more tailored look, the seam allowances may be pressed to one side.

TOPSTITCHING
Because of the nature of Ultrasuede, almost all seams and edges need stitching to help keep them flat and create a professional appearance. A lapped seam is edgestitched along both seam allowance edges. A conventional seam is topstitched on either side of the seam, or if the seam is pressed to one side, the topstitching goes through all three layers.

To successfully topstitch Ultrasuede, use a Teflon foot, a roller foot (regular or leather version), or a walking (even-feed) foot on the machine to keep the fabric feeding evenly. If you choose not to topstitch seams, use a light application of fabric glue to hold the seam allowances in place.

CLOSURES
Ultrasuede is ideal for zippered or snap closures, but it also works well with boxed or in-seam buttonholes (**figure 2**). To make a boxed buttonhole, simply straight stitch a rectangular box where you want the buttonhole and cut the center. You can also use welt buttonholes.

HEMMING

Most Ultrasuede edges are simply left raw and topstitched, as opposed to turning under a hem and creating bulk with an additional layer. On Ultrasuede Light, a traditional hem finish can be appropriate as well.

Decorative scissors or rotary blades can be used to add fun to Ultrasuede cut edges, whether in hems, along seam lines, or as trims (**figure 3**).

TRIMS

Because Ultrasuede doesn't ravel, it's perfect for cutting into fringe and other trims and edge finishing. For fringe, use scissors or a rotary cutter and ruler to slice a strip into the size and shape desired.

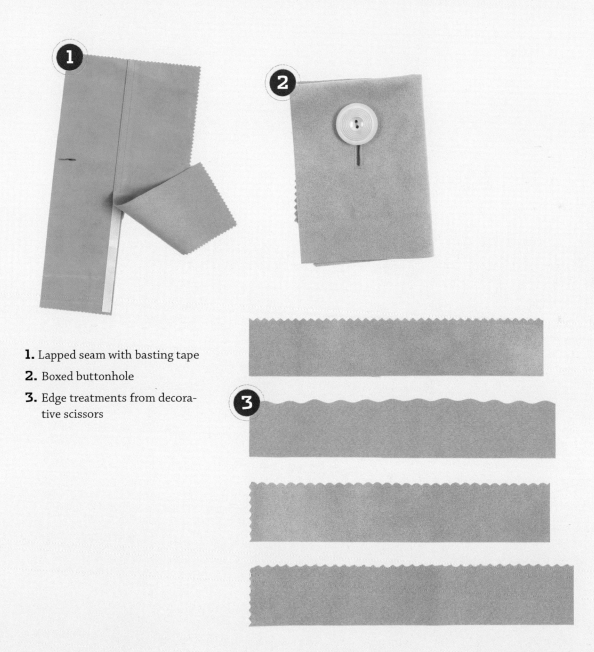

1. Lapped seam with basting tape

2. Boxed buttonhole

3. Edge treatments from decorative scissors

Little stitches make a big impact in these pretty coin purses. Try rainbow rows of back stitches or a random array of seed stitches to embellish your purse, or choose your favorite stitch patterns for a custom look. *by* RACHEL HAUSER

little stitches
COIN PURSES

FABRIC (FOR 1 PURSE)

—10" × 14" (25.5 × 35.5 cm) piece of solid cotton or linen fabric for shell (Main; *shown:* natural linen for Rainbow Purse and Moda Crossweave Blue/White for Seed Stitches Coin Purse; see Notes)

—10" × 14" (25.5 × 35.5 cm) piece of print cotton fabric for lining (Contrast)

OTHER SUPPLIES

—10" × 14" (25.5 × 35.5 cm) piece of sew-in fleece interfacing to pad purse

—Thread to match purse lining (if using a print, match the most prominent color or the background color)

—Embroidery floss: six colors (*shown:* light blue, light gray, turquoise, blue, navy blue, and dark gray) for Seed Stitches Coin Purse or 9 colors (*shown:* blue, aqua, green, lime, yellow, orange, red, burgundy, and purple) for Rainbow Purse (see Notes)

—Handsewing needle

—Embroidery or crewel needle (Crewel is a type of embroidery. Crewel needles can be found in the embroidery section and are made with larger eyes to be used with wool threads.)

—6"–8" (15–20.5 cm) embroidery hoop

—4½" × 3" (11.5 × 7.5 cm) metal purse frame

—Gutermann Creative glue (This is a specific type of glue that works well with metal.)

—Transfer paper, such as Saral, and a blunt object, such as a dry ballpoint pen (Both are optional for embroidery design transfer.)

—Table/butter knife or any type of flat, blunt object to assist you in stuffing the fabric into the purse frame during finishing

—Rag to help clean up excess glue

—Walking foot for sewing machine (optional but recommended)

—Little Stitches Coin Purse pattern on Pattern Insert

FINISHED SIZE

5½" tall × 6" wide (14 × 15 cm)

NOTES

—All seam allowances are ¼" (6 mm) unless otherwise noted.

—Fabrics with some texture add visual interest, so keep this in mind as you choose your fabric.

PREPARE AND CUT THE FABRIC

1 Prewash and dry all fabrics. You may machine-wash or handwash your fabrics, then machine-dry for best results and to preshrink natural fibers.

2 Using the provided pattern, cut the following pieces as directed. Mark the hinge notches on all pieces; do not clip.

—Cut two Purses from the interfacing

—Cut two Purses from the contrast fabric

—Cut the Main Purse pieces after completing the embroidery.

COMPLETE THE EMBROIDERY

3 Place the Main fabric right side up on your work surface (be sure to iron out any wrinkles before working with fabric, because this may affect the embroidery results). Place the Purse pattern piece on top, to one side, maintaining a 1" (2.5 cm) space from the fabric edge, and trace the piece onto the fabric. Flip the pattern piece over and position it on the remaining fabric, allowing ½" (1.3 cm) of space between the pieces and again maintaining a 1" (2.5 cm) space from the fabric edge (the extra 1" [2.5 cm] is to ensure you have enough space to place the pieces into the embroidery hoop without overlapping into your workspace). Trace the reversed Purse piece; do not cut out.

4 For the Rainbow Purse only, transfer the embroidery design onto both Main fabric Purse pieces, using your preferred transfer method, such as tracing the design with a removable fabric marker, using a light table or bright window, or using transfer paper. Using transfer paper is much like using tracing paper. Place the transfer paper between your pattern and your fabric, with the transfer side next to the fabric. Using a blunt object, such as a pencil, dry ballpoint pen, or stylus, trace over the embroidery markings. There is no embroidery design for the Seed Stitches Coin Purse.

5 Center the hoop on the desired portion of one traced Purse piece in an embroidery hoop. Choose embroidery floss and cut a piece about as long as your arm (or about 24"–30" [61–76 cm]). Divide the six-strand floss evenly, creating two lengths of three-stranded floss. Thread the needle with one three-strand length and knot the end. To stitch, come up from the wrong side of your work, pulling until the knot catches and always keeping the right side of the work facing you. When you finish any length of floss,

secure the end with a knot. Refer to the sidebar on page 46 for further embroidery instructions.

6 After completing the embroidery, press the fabric and retrace the main Purse pieces (the fabric may have stretched during embroidery). Cut out the two main Purse pieces along the traced lines.

ASSEMBLE THE SHELL AND LINING

7 Place the two Main Purse pieces right sides together. Place an interfacing Purse against each exposed wrong side of the Main Purse sandwich. You should have a stack of four layers, with the Main Purse pieces inside and the interfacing Purse pieces outside. Pin together through all layers, from one hinge notch, down and along the straight bottom edge, to the other hinge notch. Do not pin along the curved upper edge.

8 With your walking foot installed (refer to your sewing machine manual for assistance), sew from one hinge mark to the other, backtacking at the beginning and end.

9 Leaving the assembled purse wrong side out, finger-press the seam allowances open along the bottom and side of the purse at one corner. Match the side and bottom seam allowances along the seam line, creating a flattened triangle shape at the corner. To make sure the seams are accurately matched, pass a pin through the center of the seam from the bottom of the purse and check that it pokes out at the center of the seam on the other side. Use pins to stabilize the flattened triangle. Measure from the point of the triangle up along the seam line. Make a line perpendicular to the seam at ¾" (2 cm) from the triangle point. Stitch along this line, backtacking at the beginning and end. Trim the corner ¼" (6 mm) from the stitch line (**figure 1**). Repeat to box the opposite corner. You have now assembled the shell purse.

Note: If your sewing machine has trouble feeding the thick flattened triangle, start stitching about ¼" (6 mm) from the beginning of the drawn line and then backtack to secure that ¼" (6 mm).

10 Repeat Steps 7 and 8 to sew the lining (using the Contrast fabric Purse pieces and ignoring references to interfacing) but leave a 3" (7.5 cm) unstitched gap in the center of the bottom edge. Then, repeat Step 9 to box the corners. Leave the assembled lining purse inside out.

figure 1

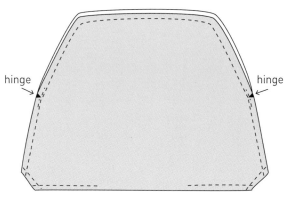

hinge   hinge

figure 2

ASSEMBLE THE PURSE

11 Place the shell purse inside the lining purse so the right sides are together, aligning the seams, the hinge notches, and the curved top edges. The portion of the purse above the hinge notches will be referred to as the purse flaps. Both purse flaps will be sewn from hinge notch to hinge notch through all three layers. If hinge points are off, separate the lining purse from the shell purse and make adjustments to correct by nudging the pieces until they match. When well matched, pin through all three layers on both purse flaps.

12 Sew each purse flap from hinge notch to hinge notch, being very careful not to leave any gaps between the stitch line and the previous seam (**figure 2**). If gaps are left, you will end up with holes at your hinge points.

13 Pull the shell purse right side out through the gap in the lining. Check that there are no holes at the hinge points. Press the purse flaps flat along the curved seam.

14 Pull the lining out of the shell and locate the gap left for turning. Turn in the raw edges ¼" (6 mm) to match the seam and pin. Handstitch closed with a slip stitch, using thread that matches the lining fabric.

FINISHING

15 Prepare to glue the purse into the purse frame by finding a flat, nonporous work surface and gathering the purse, metal purse frame, Gutermann glue, a rag, and a table/butter knife. Work in a well-ventilated area.

16 Notice that the purse flaps are wider than the frame. This is what causes the finished purse to puff out attractively. The knife will help you stuff the purse flaps into the frame neatly. Apply the glue generously to one inside track of the purse frame. Set the frame down. Wait three minutes before continuing to allow the glue to become tacky and less runny. Stuff the flap into the frame by working on the sides first and then the top, then finish by pushing in the corners. Don't worry, you don't have to work super fast (five minutes is fine). The glue comes off the frame easily after you're done, with a damp rag. However, avoid getting glue on the fabric. When the purse flap is generally in place (be sure to center the middle embroidery lines [shown in yellow on the sample] if working on the Rainbow Purse), use the knife to tuck the edges deeply into the purse frame.

17 Let the first side dry for about five minutes while rubbing off any glue that got onto the metal frame. Repeat Step 15 on the other side, waiting three minutes after applying the glue before stuffing the purse flap into the frame. Allow the glue to dry overnight in a well-ventilated area before using your finished coin purse.

SEWN *by hand*

Handsewing has been around forever. Primitive people laced skins together for garments, and creative sewers made family garb using only handstitches before the nineteenth-century invention of the sewing machine. Today, handsewing is often used for finishing and fine detailing where results demand more control than machines can give. Handstitching also makes a project portable.

If you have a daily commute or a child's softball game to attend, it's easy to tuck handwork into a carry-along bag.

GETTING READY

Many kinds of handsewing needles are available, and the one you choose will depend on the task. A sharp, however, is the needle most commonly used. Its round eye and medium length make it suitable for most stitching tasks.

You can use beeswax or other thread conditioners to add strength to handsewing threads; it also helps prevent knotting.

If you're basting, consider using silk thread because you can press over it without leaving an impression on the fabric.

Most handsewing is best done with a single thread strand, though you can double the thread for added durability and for use on heavy fabrics. The ideal thread length is less than 24" (61 cm). Thread the end that first comes off the spool through the needle's eye and tie an overhand knot at end of the thread.

To begin stitching, anchor the knot in the fabric or bury the end between two layers for an invisible start. Alternatively, take a few backstitches to secure the thread ends. It's important to keep handstitches loose enough to avoid puckering but tight enough to be secure.

COMMON STITCHES

Most stitches are worked right to left for right-handers and left to right for left-handers, though there are exceptions. Practice stitching on scraps before working on your actual project. The goal of most handsewing efforts is invisible (or minimally visible) stitches. Select a thread color that closely matches your work.

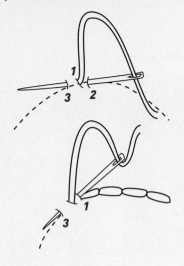

BACKSTITCH ▲

One of the strongest stitches, the backstitch is ideal for sewing and/or repairing seams, topstitching, and inserting zippers. Backstitching looks much like machine stitching, only the stitches overlap on the underside.

*To create a backstitch, bring the needle up at **1** and insert behind the starting point at **2**. Bring the needle up at **3**. Repeat by inserting at **1** and bringing the needle up at a point that is a stitch length beyond (**3**).*

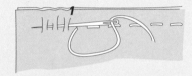

RUNNING STITCH ▲

This short even stitch can be used for seaming, mending, easing, and gathering, as well as for decoration. Longer stitches are used for basting (see above). Weave the needle in and out of the fabric several times before pulling it through. Length and spacing can vary depending whether the stitching is permanent or temporary.

*Insert the needle at **1** and, keeping the needle in the fabric, bring the needle in and out of the fabric several times, then pull the needle through. Tighten the stitches but do not pull so tightly that you pucker the fabric.*

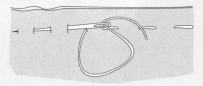

BASTING ▲

Used to temporarily hold layers together, a basting stitch is simply a long running stitch (see below). Stitches should be about ¼" (6 mm) long and evenly spaced.

WHIPSTITCH ▼

This diagonal overcasting stitch is used to join two finished edges and attach hook and eyes and snaps.

*Bring the needle up at **1**, insert at **2**, and bring up at **3**. These quick stitches do not have to be very tight or close together but can be closely spaced for things such as attaching hook and eyes.*

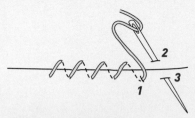

OVERCAST STITCH ▼

Used to prevent fabrics from fraying, overcast stitches can be placed close together or far apart. The diagonal stitches should be evenly spaced, however, and at a uniform distance from the edge of a single fabric layer. A hand-overcast stitch can replace machine zigzagging or serging. Place the stitches closer together on fabrics prone to fraying.

Keeping your stitches at consistent depth and spacing, take a diagonal stitch by bringing the needle through the fabric at **1**, wrapping the thread over the edge, and then bringing the needle through the fabric again at **2**, to the side of the previous stitch. The result is a diagonal stitch that wraps around the edge.

BLANKET STITCH ▼

A favorite of appliquérs and fleece sewers, the blanket stitch is used to finish the fabric edge (either singly as on fleece and felt or with the edge folded under on ravely fabrics). Work from left to right (right-handers).

*Working from left to right, bring the needle up at **1** and insert at **2** Bring the needle back up at **3** and over the working thread. Repeat by making the next stitch in the same manner, keeping the spacing even.*

NOTE: *When sewn only over thread strands, a blanket stitch is also used for French tacks, thread eyes, and belt loops.*

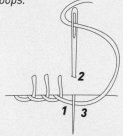

BLINDSTITCH/BLIND-HEM STITCH ▼

Sewn between the hem (or facing) and the garment, this small zigzag stitch catches only a bit of the garment fabric so no stitches show on the right side. Space the alternating stitches about ¼" (6 mm) apart.

Fold the hem edge back about ¼" (6 mm). Take a small stitch in the garment, picking up only a few threads

of the fabric, then take the next stitch about ¼" (6 mm) ahead in the hem, again picking up only a few threads. Continue, alternating stitches between the hem and garment.

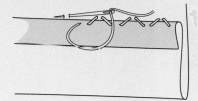

BUTTONHOLE STITCH ▼

Used for edge finishing and making hand buttonholes, this stitch looks much like a blanket stitch, but it's worked in the opposite direction.

*Working from right to left and with the point of the needle toward you, bring the needle above the fabric edge at **1**, loop the thread to the left, then down and to the right, inserting the needle from the wrong side at **2**, keeping the loop of thread behind the needle at both the top and bottom. Pull the needle through, tightening the stitch so that the looped thread lies along the edge of the fabric. Do not tighten so much that the tops of the stitches pull together.*

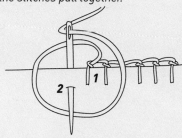

When using the buttonhole stitch to finish a hand buttonhole, work the stitches so that they are very closely spaced.

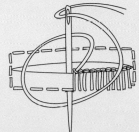

UNEVEN SLIP STITCH ▼

Mostly hidden inside a fabric fold, the uneven slip stitch works well for securing linings. A small stitch is taken on the outer fabric and the traveling stitches (between the visible ones) are inside the fabric fold. Space stitches ⅛" (3 mm) to ¼" (6 mm) apart.

After securing the thread in the fold, take a small stitch in the garment or outer fabric, picking up only a few threads of the fabric. Then, take a stitch, about ¼" (6 mm) long, in the fold, across from the stitch in the garment/outer fabric. Continue, alternating between tiny stitches in the garment/outer fabric and longer stitches in the fold.

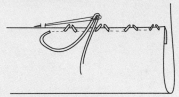

ENDING UP ▼

At the end of a line of permanent handstitching, take a small stitch and pull the needle and thread through the loop. Take another short backstitch and repeat. Clip the thread ends close to the stitches.

For basting or other temporary markings, make a single knot or simply leave a long thread end to allow for easy removal.

NOTE: *Another option is to take a small stitch on the fabric's wrong side, wrap the thread around the needle several times, then pull the needle through to secure the knot close to the fabric surface.*

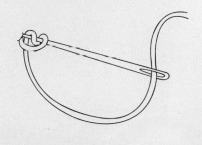

east meets west WALLET

Designer Lisa Cox paired Japanese indigo cotton prints with lightweight denim to create a stylish wallet. Three 50-yen coins stitched to the front of the wallet make a unique design accent. *by* **LISA COX**

FABRIC

—Three 10" (25.5 cm) squares of different print quilting cotton (A, B, and C; assign each fabric a letter: fabric A will be the main wallet fabric and fabrics B and C will be used for pockets and details; *shown:* Japanese indigo prints)

—⅛ yd (11.5 cm) of lightweight denim

OTHER SUPPLIES

—5" (12.5 cm) of satin piping (*shown:* cream)

—4½" × 8½" (11.5 × 21.5 cm) piece of medium-weight fusible interfacing

—Matching pearl cotton (*shown:* navy)

—Embroidery needle

—Three 50 yen Japanese coins (metal washers can be used in place of coins), about ¾" (2 cm) in diameter

—Rotary cutter, rigid acrylic ruler, and self-healing mat (optional, for cutting)

—Serger (optional)

—Zipper foot for sewing machine (optional)

FINISHED SIZE

—4" × 8" (10 × 20.5 cm) when open

—4" × 4" (10 × 10 cm) when closed

NOTE

—All seam allowances are ¼" (6 mm) unless otherwise noted.

CUT THE FABRIC

1 Cut and label the following pieces as directed (label on the wrong side with a fabric pen or tailor's chalk or use tape for temporary labels).

Fabric A:

—8½" × 4½" (21.5 × 11.5 cm) piece for Shell

—8½" × 4¼" (21.5 × 11 cm) piece for Pocket 2

Fabric B:

—8½" × 4¼" (21.5 × 11 cm) piece for Pocket 1

Fabric C:

—8½" × 8" (21.5 × 20.5 cm) piece for Pocket 3

Denim:

—4½" × 1¾" (11.5 × 4.5 cm) piece for End Panel

—8½" × 4½" (21.5 × 11.5 cm) piece for Lining

CONSTRUCT THE WALLET COVER

2 Using the denim End Panel, press under ¼" (6 mm) on one long side. With the fabric A Shell piece right side up, position the denim End Panel, right side up,

on the right-hand end of the Shell, matching up the raw edges. Tuck the raw edge of the piping in under the folded edge of the denim and pin to secure. Edgestitch on the denim to secure both the denim and the piping in place (you can use a zipper foot here if necessary to get close enough to the edge; a zipper foot was not necessary for the construction of the sample). Trim the ends of the piping flush with the Shell edges.

3 Fuse the interfacing to the wrong side of the Shell, following the manufacturer's instructions.

4 Stitch three Japanese coins (or metal washers) to the denim End Panel on the Shell, using the pearl cotton thread to secure each coin with eight evenly spaced "spoke" stitches radiating out from the hole at the center of the coin. Refer to the photo on page 48 for the placement of the coins.

CONSTRUCT THE WALLET LINING

5 Press Pockets 1 and 2 in half lengthwise with the wrong sides together so that they measure 8½" × 2⅛" (21.5 × 5.3 cm). Press Pocket 3 in half lengthwise so

✚ Insert template plastic (I sometimes reuse old x-ray films) in the base of your bag to provide structure and make it sturdy. —LISA COX

✚ Always begin a project with fabric you love. This will guarantee that you'll use and be proud of your finished project. —HEIDI BOYD

that it measures 8½" × 4" (21.5 × 10 cm). Serge or zigzag the long open edges of each pocket closed.

6 Position Pocket 2 on top of Pocket 3, so that the bottom serged/zigzagged edge of Pocket 2 is ¾" (2 cm) above the bottom edge of Pocket 3. Topstitch ⅛" (3 mm) from the bottom edge of Pocket 2 to secure it to Pocket 3 (if you finished the pocket edge with a zigzag stitch instead of serging, topstitch ¼" [6 mm] from the edge instead).

7 Position Pocket 1 on top of Pocket 3 so that the bottom serged/zigzagged edges of the two pockets are aligned. Baste the pockets together ⅛" (3 mm) from the bottom edge.

8 Mark the center of the pockets parallel to the short edges, 4¼" (11 cm) from either short edge. Stitch down the center of the pocket unit through all layers to divide the pockets into two compartments for credit cards on either side of the midline. Reinforce the midline by sewing along it once or twice more, backtacking when starting and stopping.

9 Position the pocket unit on top of the denim Lining and baste in place along the sides and bottom, ⅛" (3 mm) from the edge.

FINISH THE WALLET

10 Lay the Lining on top of the Shell with right sides together. Pin around the edges to secure.

11 Stitch around the perimeter of the wallet, leaving a 3" (7.5 cm) gap for turning on one of the long sides.

12 Clip the corners and turn right side out. Press the wallet. Fold the seam allowances in at the gap and handsew it closed with a slip stitch.

The perfect size for everyday use, this purse pairs the practicality of interior and side pockets with the stylish texture of houndstooth wool fabric and faux-leather handles. Create a striking wool-felt dahlia for the perfect fashionable accent. *by* **APRIL MOFFATT**

dahlia PURSE

FABRIC

—¾ yd (68.5 cm) of 54" (137 cm) wide home decorator–weight fabric for purse shell (Main; *shown:* Premier Prints, Large Houndstooth in Stone/Denton)

—¾ yd (68.5 cm) of 45" (114.5 cm) wide osnaburg or other cotton or linen fabric for purse lining (*shown:* natural osnaburg)

—¼ yd (23 cm) of 54" (137 cm) wide faux leather for straps (*shown:* yellow-tan embossed)

—12" × 24" (30.5 × 61 cm) piece of wool felt for dahlia flower (*shown:* National Nonwovens Wool Felt in white)

OTHER SUPPLIES

—1¼ yd (1.1 m) of 44" (112 cm wide heavyweight fusible interfacing

—Matching sewing thread

—Heavy-duty sewing needle, size 90/14 or 100/16 jeans/denim needle

—Four 1" (2.5 cm) D rings

—Hot glue gun and glue sticks

—Point turner (or similar tool, such as a chopstick)

—Large safety pin

—Bulldog clips or tape

—Water-soluble fabric marker

—Dahlia Purse pattern and templates on Pattern Insert

—*Optional:* Teflon presser foot

FINISHED SIZE

—9" high × 13" wide × 5" deep without straps (23 × 33 × 12.5 cm)

NOTES

—Seam allowances are ½" (1.3 cm) unless otherwise noted.

—Home decorator–weight fabric is recommended for this purse, because it adds much more stability and holds its shape well.

—Use a heavy-duty needle when sewing this project, such as a size 90/14 or 100/16 jeans/denim needle. The faux leather straps and the many layers of this purse need a strong needle for smooth sewing.

—A Teflon presser foot may be useful when stitching faux leather.

—Press all fabric (other than the faux leather) before beginning. Do not apply heat to the faux leather.

—If you'd like to make your own felt to create the felt dahlia, see the sidebar on page 57.

CUT THE FABRIC

Be sure to transfer all pattern markings to the fabric wrong side as you cut the following pieces.

1 Cut the following pieces as directed, using the provided pattern.

From Main fabric, cut:

—Two Purse Panels on the fold

—Two Side Panels

—Four Side Pockets

From lining fabric, cut:

—Two Purse Panels on the fold

—Two Side Panels

—Two Interior Pockets

From the faux leather, cut:

—Two rectangles, 3" × 20" (7.5 × 51 cm) for Handles

From the fusible interfacing, cut:

—Four Purse Panels on the fold

—Four Side Panels

—Four Side Pockets

—One Interior Pocket

2 Fuse the interfacing pieces to the wrong sides of the corresponding Main fabric and lining pieces, following the manufacturer's instructions.

MAKE THE PURSE ELEMENTS

3 Fold a scant ½" (1.3 cm) to the wrong side along both long edges of one Handle piece. Use clips or tape to hold the hems in place; do not use pins or press with an iron. Topstitch ¼" (6 mm) from each long edge. Turn another scant ½" (1.3 cm) to the wrong side on each long edge and topstitch ¼" (6 mm) from the new fold. Repeat to make the second Handle.

Note: The faux leather's thickness and stiffness may consume extra fabric in turning the hems. Adjust the amount of fabric folded to the wrong side as necessary for handles that finish 1" (2.5 cm) wide.

4 Stitch the two Interior Pockets right sides together, leaving an opening between the dots. Clip the corners and turn right side out. Work the corners into place with a point turner or other tool and then press the pocket flat. Edgestitch the top edge of the pocket.

5 Place one lining Purse Panel right side up on your work surface and pin the assembled interior pocket, right side up, 2" (5 cm) above the bottom edge and

centered side to side. Edgestitch the sides and bottom of the pocket. Backtack securely at the start and finish to secure the pocket. Use a removable marking tool to draw a line from top to bottom on the pocket, 2¾" (7 cm) from the pocket's right edge. Topstitch along the line to divide the pocket.

6 With two Side Pockets right sides together, stitch across the top and bottom edges only. Turn the pocket right side out and press. Topstitch the upper edge only, ¼" and ½" (6 mm and 1.3 cm) from the edge. Repeat the entire step with the remaining Side Pocket pieces.

ASSEMBLE THE SHELL AND LINING

7 Use the Main fabric pieces for the following instructions until instructed otherwise.

8 Pin one of the assembled Side Pockets to one Side Panel, right sides up, with the topstitched upper edge 2½" (6.5 cm) below the panel's upper edge. Stitch across the bottom edge of the pocket, ¼" (6 mm) from the edge. Baste the side edges of the pocket to the panel, ⅜" (1 cm) from the raw edges. Repeat the entire step with the remaining side pocket and Side Panel. These assembled pieces will now be referred to as side panels.

9 Place the two side panels right sides together and stitch the center bottom seam. Press the seam allowances open. Place the seamed side panels on one Purse Panel, right sides together, aligning the seam with the center bottom notch on the Purse Panel; pin together between the dots only. Stitch between the dots. Clip the side panel seam allowance at the dots, clipping to, but not through, the stitches. This releases the side panel seam allowance for turning the corners.

10 Position one Side Panel along the side of the Purse Panel, matching the raw edges. Pin together, making sure that the side pockets are flat. Starting at the corner, stitch to the upper edge. Repeat to attach the other Side Panel to the remaining side edge of the Purse Panel.

11 Repeat Steps 8 and 9 to stitch the free edge of the side panels to the remaining Purse Panel, and then turn the purse right side out. Press all seam allowances open as well as you can to complete the purse shell.

12 Repeat Steps 8–10 with the lining pieces to assemble the purse lining, ignoring references to the side pockets. Leave a 4" (10 cm) opening in one side panel/purse panel seam near the center bottom. Leave the lining wrong side out.

✚ When designing bags with pocket panels, I like to minimize seams by cutting an extra-long main panel and accordion-folding the pockets into it. It takes just a quick press with an iron and a topstitched divider or two to make sturdy self-lined pockets. —KEVIN KOSBAB

FINISH THE PURSE ASSEMBLY

13 With the shell purse right side out and the lining purse wrong side out, slide the lining over the shell, aligning all seams; right sides will be together. Pin and then stitch all the way around the top edge. Trim the corners and clip the curves. Carefully pull the shell purse through the opening in the lining to turn the bag right side out. Using a point turner or similar tool, work all the corners and edges into place. Press the top edge of the purse well. Topstitch the top edge of the purse ¼" (6 mm) from the edge.

14 Slip one end of one Handle through a D ring. Fold 1" (2.5 cm) of Handle fabric to the wrong side and edgestitch to the Handle, enclosing the D ring. Repeat this process with both ends of each Handle.

15 Making sure that the right side of the Handle is facing out, wrap the narrow tab at the top of one purse side through a Handle D ring from front to back. Fold ½" (1.3 cm) to the wrong side and edgestitch to the pocket front, enclosing the D ring. Repeat to attach the Handles to the other three tabs, one Handle on the purse front and one on the purse back. Make sure that all the purse tabs are folded and stitched equally.

CREATE THE DAHLIA EMBELLISHMENT

16 Use the templates at right to cut the following from the felt:

—Twenty Large Petals

—Sixteen Medium Petals

—One Circle

—One strip, 3" × 20" (7.5 × 51 cm)

17 Fold the felt strip in half lengthwise and make clips ½" (1.3 cm) deep into the folded edge every ¼" (6 mm). Starting at one end, roll the folded strip to make the flower center. Stop every few inches to secure the roll with a needle and thread. Allow successive rows of clipped felt to lie a bit lower than the previous rows, forming a rounded half-ball. Continue rolling the strip and securing with a needle and thread until the entire strip is secured.

18 Fold the sides of one petal toward the center of the right side so that they overlap slightly, making the petal base about ¾" (2 cm) wide (**figure 1**). Secure with a dot of hot glue near the base. Repeat with all the remaining petals of both sizes. When all the petals have cooled, start gluing the Large Petals in place, overlapping the outer rim of the felt Circle ¼" (6 mm). Next, glue the Medium Petals to the Large Petals, with their bases roughly matched. Handsew the rolled strip to the center of the circle, covering the petals' bases. Use a large safety pin to secure the flower to the outside of the purse so that it can be changed out. Enjoy!

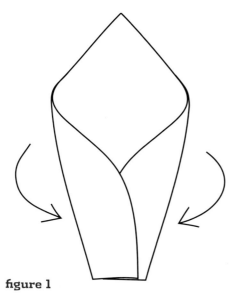

figure 1

TEMPLATES

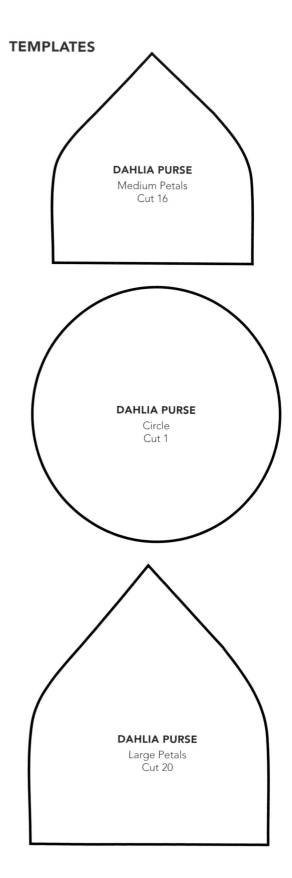

DAHLIA PURSE
Medium Petals
Cut 16

DAHLIA PURSE
Circle
Cut 1

DAHLIA PURSE
Large Petals
Cut 20

DIY *felting*

Felting is a great way to recycle garments with a wool fiber content of at least 50% to create new projects. The higher the wool content, the more the fabric can felt. Look for cashmere, merino, and other animal-hair fibers. Depending on the look that you want for your finished project, you can use flat, cabled, or otherwise patterned knits; patterned wovens; or heathered wools. Technically, the wet-felting process described here is called fulling; the fabric shrinks and the yarns interlock to create a thicker (fuller), nonraveling material.

HOW TO CREATE FELTED WOOL FABRIC FROM WOOL SWEATERS

- To disassemble sweaters in preparation for felting, carefully cut off the sleeves at the armhole seams. Cut the sleeves open by cutting along each underarm seam. Cut the shoulder seams open from the armhole to the neckline. On each sweater, cut along one of the sweater's side seams to open it flat. If you do not want the other side seam to be a part of your fabric, cut it off, too. The edges of fine or lightweight knits may need to be zigzagged or serged to prevent raveling before the felting is complete.

- Three factors are essential for felting to occur: heat (choose a hot setting on your washing machine), agitation (choose a setting appropriate for heavily soiled clothes), and moisture. Agitation locks the scales along the fiber surface together, and the moisture and heat facilitate the felting (fulling) process. Adding a little detergent to the mix assists in felting the fibers.

- Monitor the fabric during felting and stop the process when the wool is sufficiently felted; once the fibers interlock the process is irreversible, so don't allow the material to shrink too much. If the wool comes out of the washing cycle felted to your satisfaction, you may lay it flat to dry. Otherwise, to achieve greater density, toss the wool in the dryer, set at a warm or hot temperature.

FELTING TIPS

- Cutting off hems, seams, and ribbing/ribbed bands eliminates puckering and makes the fabric lie flatter.

- Felted wool does not fray, so finishing raw edges is not required (the exception to this is that lightweight knits may require an edge finish prior to felting to control raveling).

- Knitted garments tend to have the most stretch going around the body (in the crosswise direction), so if your knits are only lightly felted (i.e., some stitch definition remains) keep that in mind when you plan and lay out your patterns for felted fabric projects. If your knits are fully felted, this won't be a factor in cutting patterns.

pretty petals CLUTCH

Make a one-of-a-kind accessory with a kaleidoscope of fabrics from your sewing stash. Featuring fused appliquéd petals and a handful of sewn-on buttons, this small clutch's fun embellishments make a big impression. *by* **REBEKA LAMBERT**

FABRIC

—¼ yd (23 cm) of 45" (114.5 cm) wide natural-colored linen for shell (Main)

—¼ yd (23 cm) of 45" (114.5 cm) wide print cotton for lining (Contrast)

—Thirty scraps of various coordinating prints, each at least 1" × 2" (2.5 × 5 cm; or use fewer, but larger, scraps) for appliqué

OTHER SUPPLIES

—¼ yd (23 cm) of 27" (68.5 cm) wide sew-in ultra-firm interfacing

—9" × 12" (23 × 30.5 cm) sheet of fusible web

—Matching sewing thread

—Sewing thread to coordinate with appliqué fabrics (optional, see Step 9)

—½" (1.3 cm) magnetic snap

—Twelve to twenty buttons in various sizes, ⅜" to ⅞" (10–22 mm)

—Removable fabric marking pen

—Handsewing needle

—Appliqué Clutch pattern and template on Pattern Insert

FINISHED SIZE

6" (15 cm) tall × 11" (28 cm) wide × 2" (5 cm) deep.

NOTES

—Seam allowances are ⅜" (1 cm), unless otherwise indicated.

—A fusible interfacing can be substituted for the sew-in interfacing.

—The fusible appliqué technique does not require additional stitching; however, decorative stitching can be added just inside the petal edges, if desired.

CUT THE FABRIC

1 Using the provided pattern, cut two Bag Body pieces each from the Main fabric, Contrast fabric, and interfacing. Cut one Bag Flap each from the Main fabric and Contrast fabric, and two from the interfacing. Cut a 3½" × 2½" (9 × 6.5 cm) rectangle from the Contrast fabric for the flower center.

PREPARE THE APPLIQUÉ

2 Cut a 3½" × 2½" (9 × 6.5 cm) rectangle from the fusible web. Following the manufacturer's instructions, adhere the fusible web to the wrong side of the same-size Contrast rectangle.

3 Using the Flower Center template, trace the flower center onto the fusible web's release paper and cut along the traced outline; set aside.

4 Using the Petal template, trace thirty petals onto the paper side of the remaining fusible web. Roughly cut the petals about ⅛" (3 mm) outside the traced outline. Place each traced petal on the wrong side of a fabric scrap and fuse. Cut out each petal along the traced outline, then remove the paper backing from the petals.

APPLY THE APPLIQUÉ

5 Transfer the petal row guidelines from the Bag Body pattern to the right side of one Main fabric piece using removable fabric marking pen.

6 Starting ⅜" (1 cm) from one end of the outermost placement line, align the straight side of one petal with the guideline. Continue placing petals, side by side, until you have filled the line; you will use eleven petal pieces. Adjust the spacing, if necessary, by allowing space between petals or overlapping adjacent petals. Remember not to position petals within the seam allowance at the bag top. Fuse the row of petals in place.

7 Repeat Step 6 with the middle row, then the innermost row. Use ten petals for the middle row and nine petals for the inner row.

8 Next, remove the paper backing from the flower center, aligning its straight edge with the top edge of the bag and covering the straight edges of the innermost row of petals. Fuse in place.

9 If desired, topstitch around the flower center, close to the edge. Additional rows of stitching can be added along each row of petals, if desired.

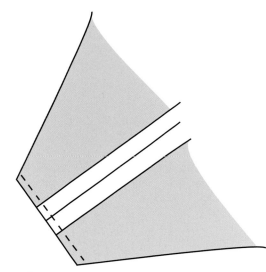

figure 1

PREPARE THE BAG CLOSURE

10 Pin baste one piece of the Bag Flap interfacing to the wrong side of the Contrast fabric Bag Flap.

11 Transfer the magnetic snap location indicated on the pattern to the right side of the flap lining (Contrast fabric). Following the manufacturer's instructions, insert the male half of the magnetic snap through both layers at the mark.

12 Pin baste the remaining Bag Flap interfacing to the wrong side of the Main fabric Bag Flap. Place the Bag Flap pieces right sides together, aligning the raw edges. Sew around the flap using a ¼" (6 mm) seam allowance, leaving the straight edge open. Turn the flap right side out.

13 Pin baste a piece of interfacing to the wrong side of the appliquéd Bag Body. Transfer the magnetic snap location from the template to the flower center's right side and insert the second half of the snap at the location through all layers.

ASSEMBLE THE BAG BODY

14 Pin baste the remaining Bag Body interfacing to the wrong side of the bag back (the unembellished Bag Body). Place the Bag Bodies right sides together, aligning the raw edges. Sew the side seams and the bottom seam.

15 Fold the bag right sides together so one side seam is aligned with the bottom seam and the corner cutout edges meet in a straight line. Sew the corner seam (**figure 1**). Repeat the entire step at the other corner.

16 Repeat Steps 14 and 15 for the bag lining, omitting the interfacing layer. Leave a 5" (12.5 cm) opening in the lining bottom seam for turning.

ASSEMBLE THE BAG

17 Pin the Bag Flap to the shell bag back, right sides together (linen against linen). Position the flap between the notches on the bag back and align the raw edges.

18 With the bag shell wrong side out and the lining right side out, insert the lining into the bag shell, with the flap between the bag layers. Align the top edges of the shell and lining, matching the side seams, and pin in place.

19 Sew the bag to the lining around the entire top.

20 Reach through the opening in the lining to turn the bag right side out, pulling the flap away from the bag and lining. Close the gap in the lining seam with hand or machine stitches, then smooth the lining inside the bag. Press.

21 Topstitch around the top of the bag, ¼" (6 mm) from the edge.

22 Arrange a variety of buttons to cover the entire surface of the flap. With matching or coordinating thread, handsew the buttons to the flap. Hide knots under the buttons, or slip them between the flap layers, and sew through only the upper fabric layer and interfacing so the stitches aren't visible on the flap lining.

Combine appliqué, decorative stitching, and brightly colored heavyweight linen to create a one-of-a-kind bag that is pretty and practical. The drawstring closure ensures easy access plus plenty of room for carrying all your necessities. *by* **CAROL ZENTGRAF**

appliqué linen DRAWSTRING HANDBAG

FABRIC

—¾ yd (68.5 cm) of 54" (137 cm) wide heavyweight linen

—½ yd (45.5 cm) of 45" (114.5 cm) wide cotton fabric for lining

OTHER SUPPLIES

—1 yd (91.5 cm) of 20" (51 cm) wide medium-to heavyweight fusible interfacing

—Two 9" × 12" (23 × 30.5 cm) sheets of double-sided fusible web (such as Steam-A-Seam 2®)

—Sewing thread in contrasting color

—7 yd (6.4 m) of ½" (1.3 cm) wide double-fold bias tape

—Rotary cutter, rigid acrylic ruler, and self-healing mat

—Vine appliqué template on pattern insert

—Flower appliqué template on pattern insert

—One ⅜" (1 cm) button

FINISHED SIZE

18½" × 14½" (47 × 37 cm) excluding straps

CUT AND PREPARE THE FABRIC

1 Cut the following pieces as directed.

From the heavyweight linen:

— Two 14½" × 18½" (37 × 47 cm) rectangles for the Front and Back Panels

— One 6" × 12" (15 × 30.5 cm) rectangle for the Pocket

— Two 6" × 20" (15 × 51 cm) strips for the Handles

From the cotton lining fabric:

— Two 14½" × 18½" (37 × 47 cm) rectangles

From the fusible interfacing:

— Two 14½" × 18½" (37 × 47 cm) rectangles

2 Trace the Vine Appliqué pattern from the pattern insert onto one sheet of double-sided fusible web; reverse the pattern and trace on the second sheet. Trace Flower Appliqué pattern onto one of these sheets. Follow the manufacturer's instructions to apply the fusible web to the wrong side of the remaining linen fabric. Cut out the appliqué motifs, but do not remove the paper backing.

ASSEMBLE THE BAG

3 Following the manufacturer's instructions, fuse the interfacing to the wrong sides of the Front and Back linen Panels.

4 To make the Pocket, press the pocket rectangle fabric in half with wrong sides together to make a 6" (15 cm) square. Cut 19" (48.5 cm) of double fold bias tape. Folding ends under and mitering corners, wrap bias tape around the three raw edges of the Pocket and edgestitch ⅛" (3 mm) from the inside edge. Using contrasting thread, sew a decorative stitch along the top folded edge and the two sides of the Pocket.

5 Remove the paper backing from the Flower Appliqué and fuse it to the center of the Pocket 1½" (3.8 cm) above the bottom edge. Blanket stitch the appliqué in place. Use straight stitches to add leaves and a flourish under the pocket. Sew the button at the base of the flower.

6 Center the Pocket 1½" (3.8 cm) above the bottom raw edge of the Front panel. Blanket stitch the sides and bottom edge in place.

7 Remove the paper backing from the Vine Appliqués. Referring to photo for placement and aligning the bottom of the stems with the bottom edge of the panel, fuse the appliqués to the Front Panel. Blanket stitch the appliqués in place. Use a straight stitch to add lines of decorative stitching around the appliqués.

8 Press the short edges of each Handle strip under ½" (1.3 cm) to the wrong side. Fold each strip in half vertically and press (**figure 1a**). Open the strip up and fold each long edge in toward the center to meet at the crease and press (**figure 1b**). Fold the strip in half again along the first fold line and press. Topstitch each long side ⅛" (3 mm) from the folded edges (**figure 1c**).

9 With wrong sides together and matching raw edges, baste the Front linen panel to a lining panel. Mitering the corners, wrap bias tape around all four edges of the Panel and edgestitch ⅛" (3 mm) from the inside edge of the bias tape. Repeat with Back Panel.

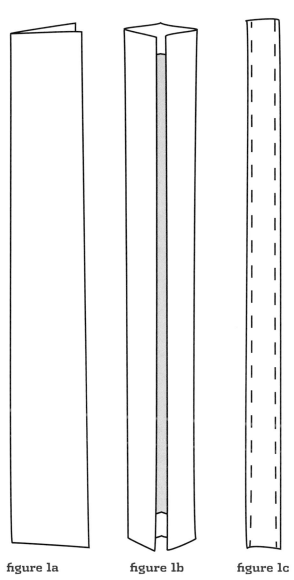

figure 1a   figure 1b   figure 1c

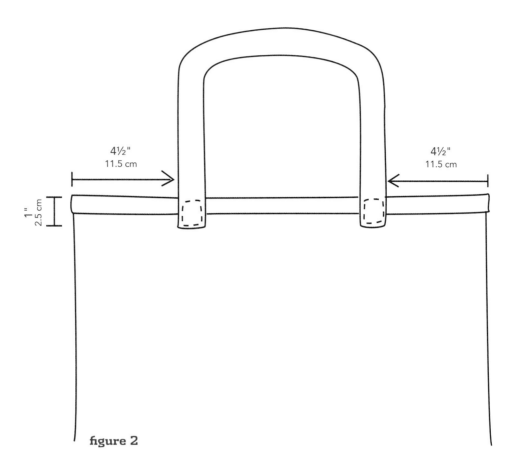

4½"
11.5 cm

4½"
11.5 cm

1"
2.5 cm

figure 2

10 With the lining sides facing and edges even, sew the Front and Back together along the inside edges of the bias tape on the bottom and sides.

11 Turn the bag inside out. Pin the handles to the Front and Back 4½" (11.5 cm) from each side with the ends extending 1" (2.5 cm) past the top edge. Edgestitch a square to secure the end of the strap (**figure 2**).

12 To make a 1" (2.5 cm) wide drawstring casing, cut a 38" (96.5 cm) length of bias tape. Open the bias tape and press the short ends under 1" (2.5 cm) (**figure 3a**); fold the tape back down to measure 1" (2.5 cm) wide (**figure 3b**). Place the bias tape around the bag 1½" (3.8 cm) from the top edge so that the folded ends meet in the center of the back bag panel; pin in place. Topstitch ⅛" (3 mm) inside both long edges on the back side of bag and leave the short edges open for the drawstring (**figure 4**); topstitch the long edges of the casing down on the front side of the bag.

13 To make a ½" (1.3 cm) wide drawstring, cut a 48" (122 cm) length of bias tape and stitch the open long edge closed with an edgestitch. Use a safety pin to feed one end through the casing. Tie each end in an overhand knot.

14 Turn the bag right side out. Pull the drawstring on the inside of the bag to gather as desired and tie the drawstring ends into a bow.

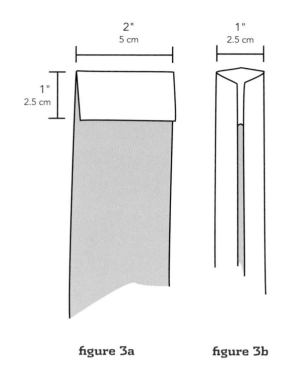

2"
5 cm

1"
2.5 cm

1"
2.5 cm

figure 3a

figure 3b

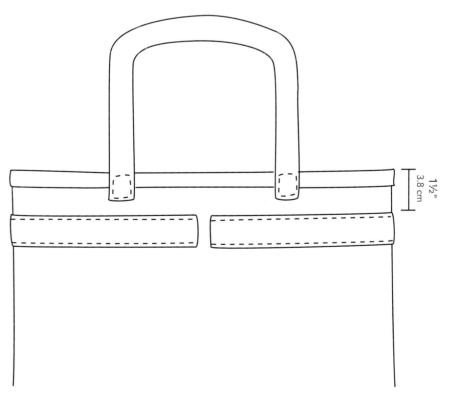

1½"
3.8 cm

figure 4

Buttons, trims, appliqué, and embroidery combine to make these whimsical, zippered pouches sewn with colorful prints. The cotton fabric body is backed with fusible interfacing for structure and lined in coordinating fabrics.

by **HEIDI BOYD**

zippy POUCHES

FABRIC (for one pouch)

—¼ yd (23 cm) each of three coordinating print fabrics (see Notes)

OTHER SUPPLIES

—¼ yd (23 cm) medium weight fusible interfacing

—9" (23 cm) zipper

—Sewing thread in three or four coordinating colors

—Fusible web

—6" (15 cm) fine silk cord for zipper pull

—One ¾" (2 cm) and one ½" (1.3 cm) felt bead (*shown:* red and white; can be found at artbeads.com) for zipper pull

—Clear-drying craft glue or seam sealant

—Zipper foot for sewing machine

—Crewel (embroidery) and handsewing needles

—Zippy Pouches pattern and appliqué templates on pattern insert

HEDGEHOG & FLOWERS

—3" × 4" (7.5 × 10 cm) off-white (or desired color) linen scrap for Hedgehog appliqué

—6" (15 cm) of ¼" (6 mm) wide picot-edged satin ribbon (*shown:* muted green)

—Brown and green (or desired colors) embroidery floss

—¼ yd (23 cm) of 1½" (3.8 cm) wide pleated ribbon trim (*shown:* taupe)

—Two ¼" (6 mm) round plastic buttons (*shown:* shades of brown)

—1½" × ⅞" (1.3 × 2.2 cm) wooden leaf button

TRIO OF MUSHROOMS

—2" × 4" (5 × 10 cm) off-white (or desired color) linen scrap for Mushroom stem appliqués

—10" (25.5 cm) of ¼" (6 mm) wide picot-edged satin ribbon (*shown:* muted green)

—Miniature flower buttons (*shown:* three ³⁄₁₆" [5 mm]

buttons and two ⅜" [10 mm] buttons)

—Green (or desired color) embroidery floss

FINISHED SIZE

9" (23 cm) wide × 5¼" (13.5 cm) high × 1¾" (4.5 cm) deep.

NOTES

—All seam allowances are ¼" (6 mm) unless otherwise indicated.

CUT AND PREPARE FABRIC

1 Using the provided pattern, cut the following pieces as directed.

The three main fabrics are interchangeable, so use each for the pieces of your choice. Pouches shown have all three fabrics on the shell (one for the front, one for the back, and one for the gusset) and two fabrics in the lining (one for the front and back, and one for the gusset). Save scraps for making the appliqués.

—Four Bag Body (two for shell, two for lining)

—Two Gussets on fold (one for shell, one for lining)

From interfacing (use inner ["interfacing"] cut lines):

—Two Bag Body

—One Gusset on fold

2 Center each interfacing piece, adhesive side down, on the wrong side of the corresponding shell fabric pieces and, following the manufacturer's instructions, fuse the interfacing to the fabric.

EMBELLISH AND ASSEMBLE POUCH

3 On the shell Body pieces, fold the top edge ¼" (6 mm) toward the wrong side, over the interfacing, and press. With right sides facing up, pin the folded

edges of the Body pieces to the zipper tape (one on each side), ⅛" (3 mm) from the zipper teeth. Using the zipper foot on your machine, edgestitch the pieces in place (**figure 1**).

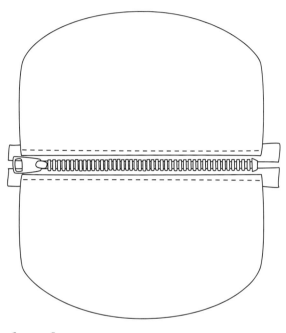

figure 1

4 Using the templates provided, trace the appliqué shapes for either the Hedgehog and Flowers or the Trio of Mushrooms onto the paper surface of the fusible web. Cut out the shapes roughly, leaving a margin around the traced outlines. Position the fusible web shapes on the wrong sides of the linen scrap and the leftover print fabric you'd like to use for the appliqués, referring to the templates for the fabric type used for each piece. Following the manufacturer's instructions, fuse the web to the fabric wrong side. Cut out each shape on the traced outline and remove the paper backing. Refer to the sidebar on page 74 to complete the embellishments for either of the appliqué sets or embellish as you desire.

5 Unzip the zipper halfway and fold the shell in half, right sides together, along the zipper. Pin the Gusset to the Bag Body and stitch the Gusset in place. Reinforce the seams by stitching again ⅛" (3 mm) from the raw edges, then trim the excess fabric close to the second row of stitches.

6 Repeat Step 5 with the lining pieces, ignoring references to the zipper. Use a ⅜" (1 cm) seam allowance to make the lining slightly smaller than the shell. Stitch

again ¼" (6 mm) from the raw edges, then trim the fabric close to the second row of stitches and turn the lining right side out. Press ¼" (6 mm) to the wrong side along the lining upper edge.

7 Pull the lining over the pouch shell so that the wrong sides are together. Match the pressed edge of the lining to the stitches along the zipper and slip stitch the lining to the zipper tapes. Tuck the Gusset ends down between the pouch layers. Handstitch them together near the zipper pull, tucking in the ends of the zipper tape, and to the base of the zipper on the other side. Turn the finished pouch right side out through the opened zipper.

8 Loop the silk cord through the zipper pull and use the crewel needle to string the two felt beads onto the cord. Remove the needle, thread it onto the other end of the cord, and pass it through the beads again. Tie both cord ends together in an overhand knot. Tie a second knot for extra security, if necessary. Trim the cord ends and add a touch of clear-drying craft glue or seam sealant to prevent raveling. Another dot of glue will further secure the knot in the cord.

EMBELLISHMENTS

Refer to photos on page 68 for assistance with placement.

FLOWERS AND HEDGEHOG

9 Cut the ¼" (6 mm) wide ribbon into two lengths, one slightly shorter than the other. Position the two lengths of ribbon vertically on one side of the pouch front so that the bottoms of the ribbon are flush with the bottom raw edge of the pouch. Temporarily place the Flower appliqué shapes (from Step 4 of the project instructions) on top of the ribbon stems to ensure the stems' placement leaves sufficient room for both Flowers. Remove the Flowers and, using coordinating thread, topstitch down the center of each ribbon to secure the stems in place. Trim any excess ribbon length.

10 Set your machine for a zigzag stitch, 2.0 mm wide and 0.3–0.4 mm long. Test the stitch on interfaced fabric scraps to determine the ideal length and width settings before stitching on the pouch. Place the Hedgehog beside the Flower stems, remembering to allow for the seams at the sides and bottom, and fuse the Hedgehog to the pouch. Position the center of the presser foot along the cut fabric edge so that the zigzag stitch spans from the appliqué to the pouch fabric, trapping the cut edge in the center of the stitch. Using a matching or coordinating color of sewing thread, stitch carefully around the perimeter of the Hedgehog, pivoting frequently around the curves. Repeat this process to attach each of the Flowers, making sure the Flowers overlap the tops of the ribbon stems, and switching thread colors to coordinate with the Flower appliqués.

11 To make the Hedgehog's spines, cut three 2" (5 cm) lengths of the pleated ribbon trim. Starting with one length of trim, fold one side of the pleats

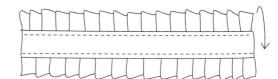

figure 2

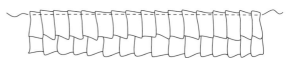

figure 3

over the central ribbon so all that's visible is a double tier of pleats (**figure 2**). Edgestitch along the fold to keep the pleats in place (**figure 3**). Repeat the process with the remaining two sections. Beginning with the strip farthest from the Hedgehog's nose, handstitch the prepared trim pieces to the appliqué. Each strip should slightly overlap the strip before it, and the fold of the final strip should fall near the leading edge of the Hedgehog's front paw.

12 Using a handsewing needle and coordinating thread, stitch on the button eye, nose, and leaf, referring to the photo for placement. Use three strands of brown (or desired color) embroidery floss and a crewel needle to embroider a smiling mouth on the Hedgehog, using a backstitch.

TRIO OF MUSHROOMS

13 Place the ¼" (6 mm) wide ribbon horizontally across the lower third of the front pouch, 1¼" (3.2 cm) above the bottom raw edge. Use coordinating thread to topstitch down the center of the ribbon. Trim the ribbon ends to match the sides of the pouch.

14 Repeat Step 10 of the Flower and Hedgehog instructions previously, to attach the trio of Mush-

rooms, beginning with the stems. Be sure to place them far enough apart to accommodate each of the Mushroom caps, referring to the photo above for placement. Position the Mushroom caps to overlap the stems a bit.

15 Use a handsewing needle and coordinating thread to sew on the Flower buttons. Finish by using three strands of green (or desired color) embroidery floss and a crewel needle to embroider blades of grass around the Mushroom stems as desired (or see photo), using long straight stitches.

APPLIQUÉ
basics

Appliqué is a fun way to add a little extra pizzazz to a sewing project or to update an existing garment or home décor item. To get you started, here are a few commonly used techniques for preparing and attaching appliqué.

RAW-EDGE METHOD
This appliqué method is quick and easy, resulting in a raw-edge finish. It's great for creating an organic and slightly frayed look with woven fabrics. It's also a great method to use with felt, faux suede, and similar fabrics that don't fray along cut edges.

You will need:

- Paper-backed fusible web (if the project calls for it or you'd like to use it)
- Pins or basting glue (if you're not using fusible web)
- Craft/paper scissors
- Fabric shears
- Embroidery scissors
- Pencil
- Handsewing needle, size 11 or 12 Sharp
- Coordinating thread or embroidery floss (for handsewing) or coordinating thread for machine sewing
- *Optional:* thimble

Remember that any time you're transferring a template to the wrong side of the fabric (or onto the paper side of the fusible web) the final appliqué will be the reverse of the traced appliqué.

figure 1

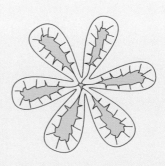

figure 2

figure 3

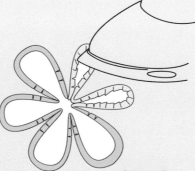

figure 4

1 Trace the template onto the paper side of the paper-backed fusible web (or trace the template onto the wrong side of the fabric or as directed by the project instructions).

2 Rough cut the shape from the fusible web, leaving a margin of about ¼" (6 mm) around the shape (if you're not using fusible web, simply cut the shape along the drawn lines). Following manufacturer's instructions, adhere the fusible web to the wrong side of the fabric and let it cool. Then, cut the shape along the drawn lines.

3 Remove the paper backing and place the shape, right side up, onto the background fabric. Adhere the shape to the background fabric as before (if you're not using fusible web, use pins or basting glue to secure the shape in place on the background fabric).

4 Stitch the shape in place around the edges, using a machine stitch, such as a straight stitch, zigzag, blanket stitch, satin stitch, or other decorative stitch (refer to your sewing machine manual for assistance). Alternatively, sew the appliqué in place using your favorite hand embroidery stitch, such as a blanket stitch, running stitch, or backstitch.

NEEDLE-TURN METHOD

Requiring minimal preparation for a turned-under edge, this method starts with the appliqué edges left raw. You then turn the edges under as you stitch the appliqué in place.

You will need:

- Pins or basting glue
- Fabric marking pen or tailor's chalk
- Fabric shears
- Embroidery scissors
- Handsewing needle, size 11 or 12 Sharp
- Lightweight cotton or silk thread
- *Optional:* thimble

1 Trace the template onto the right side of the chosen fabric, using a fabric marking pen or tailor's chalk. Cut out the shape a scant ¼" (6 mm) from the traced line.

2 Using the embroidery scissors, clip into the seam allowance at any concave curves and points (you may also clip the convex curves if doing so will make it easier for you to fold under the seam allowance neatly; **figure 1**).

3 Pin or glue-baste the appliqué to the background fabric, overlapping pieces as necessary or directed. (To glue-baste, use small dots of glue on the wrong side of the appliqué, about ¼" (6 mm) from the drawn line, to secure the appliqué to the background fabric.)

4 Use the standard hand-appliqué stitch for a neat, nearly invisible finish. As you sew, use the needle to sweep under the seam allowance just ahead of your stitching **(figure 2)**. Make sure the traced line isn't visible. Note that where appliqués overlap, the lower piece does not need to be sewn or turned under.

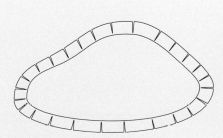

figure 1

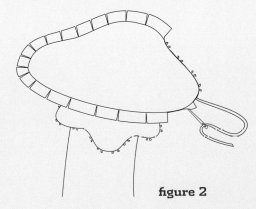

figure 2

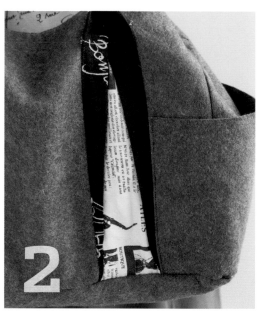

....fun techniques & materials to expand your skills

mix it UP!

If you want bags with creative construction, fun shapes, and specialty fabrics, then this is the section for you. You'll create a unique statement bag, but you'll also learn new skills along the way. Make the **1. Gadget Messenger Bag** (page 108), designed to keep you fully plugged in. Use pleated insets for a surprise pop of color in the **2. Pleats Please Bag** (page 116). Make a signature coordinated three-bag set with home décor fabric in the **3. Weekend Travel Ensemble** (page 94). Play with angles in the **4. Side-Slung Bag** (page 102). Combine cutouts, asymmetry, and appliqué to make the cool **5. Drop-Top Messenger Bag** (page 88). Sew the perfect bag accessory constructed to organize all your necessities in the **6. Charming Checkbook Cover** (page 84). Finally, learn tips and tricks for sewing with faux leather and hardware with the **7. Faux-Leather Slouch Bag** (page 78). Be fashion-forward and sew a bag that will get you noticed!

faux-leather
SLOUCH BAG

Create a stylish slouch bag for a fraction of the retail cost using supple faux leather and heavy-metal hardware. The roomy, pleated construction and cool design details make this bag look anything but handmade. *by* **BRETT BARA**

FABRIC
—1 yd (91.5 cm) of 54" (137 cm) wide light- to medium-weight faux leather or vinyl
—¾ yd (68.5 cm) 45" (114.5 cm) wide fabric for lining

OTHER SUPPLIES
—Sewing thread to match faux leather
—Four 2" (5 cm) rectangle rings (*Note:* The rectangle rings shown are approximately 2½" (6.5 cm) wide.)
—Eight ½" (1.3 cm) domed screw-in studs or similar embellishments
—Rotary cutter, rigid acrylic ruler, and self-healing mat
—Clapper or hardcover book
—Non-stick or roller sewing machine foot
—Binder clips, Wonder Clips, or basting tape
—Small Microtex (sharp) sewing machine needle or heavyweight needle

—Press cloth
—Fine-line permanent marker or pen
—Handsewing needle

FINISHED SIZE
15" × 13" × 3" (38 × 33 × 7.5 cm) excluding handles.

NOTES
—Do not iron directly on the surface of faux leather or vinyl, because it will melt. Instead, press only on the wrong side (knit backing) using a medium heat setting and a press cloth. Apply the iron for only a few seconds. Remove the iron and press firmly on the warm area with a clapper or hardcover book to allow the heat to penetrate the material without risk of melting. To avoid using an iron altogether, use a clapper or hardcover book to flatten seams open or to one side.

—Use caution when pinning, as pins will leave permanent marks. Pin only in seam allowances, or use clips or basting tape to hold seam allowances together.
—Use a small Microtex (sharp) sewing machine needle to minimize visible needle holes.
—For best results use a non-stick or roller sewing machine foot to keep the fabric moving evenly.

CUT THE FABRIC

1 Cut the following pieces as directed.

From the faux leather:

— Two 12" × 24" (30.5 × 61 cm) rectangles for the Front/Back panels. On each, cut a 2" (5 cm) square from the bottom corners (**figure 1**).

— Four 4" × 16" (10 × 40.5 cm) rectangles for Facings

— Four 7" × 8" (18 × 20.5 cm) rectangles for Tabs

— One 7" (18 cm) × width of the fabric strip. Cut this strip in half to create two straps.

From the lining fabric:

— Two 12" × 24" (30.5 × 61 cm) rectangles for the Lining pieces. On each, cut a 2" (5 cm) square from the bottom corners (**figure 1**).

MAKE THE PLEATS

2 Beginning at the top left of one Front/Back panel, measure 5" (12.5 cm) to the right and make the first mark. Make a mark every 2" (5 cm) for a total of eight marks across. The last mark should fall 5" (12.5 cm) from the right edge of the fabric (**figure 1**).

3 Fold the first mark on the left to meet the second, then fold the third mark to meet the fourth. Working from the right, fold the eighth mark to meet the seventh, then fold the sixth mark to meet the fifth. Press pleats in place using faux-leather pressing techniques.

All pleats should point toward the center with a 2" (5 cm) space between each pleat (**figure 2**).

4 Using clips to hold the pleats in place, stitch across the top ¼" (6 mm) from the edge to secure.

5 Repeat Steps 2, 3 and 4 to pleat the second Front/Back panel.

ASSEMBLE THE BAG EXTERIOR

6 With right sides together, sew one facing piece to the pleated edge of each Front/Back panel using a ½" (1.3 cm) seam allowance. Press the seam allowance toward the facing using faux leather pressing techniques, and then topstitch the facing ¼" (6 mm) from the seam line.

7 Place the Front and Back panels together with right sides facing. Sew the two side edges and bottom edge with a ½" (1.3 cm) seam allowance, leaving the corners open (**figure 3**). Press the seams open.

8 To sew each corner, match the center seams of the side and bottom with right sides together and raw edges aligned. Sew across the side/bottom seams with a ½" (1.3 cm) seam allowance (**figure 4**).

9 Fold each Tab piece in half vertically and press (**figure 5a**). Open the tab up and fold each long edge in toward the center to meet at the crease and press (**figure 5b**). Fold the piece in half again along the first

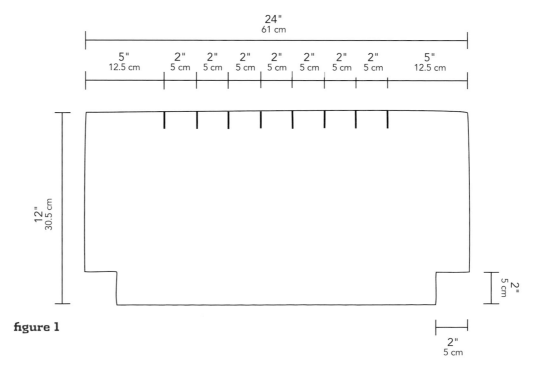

figure 1

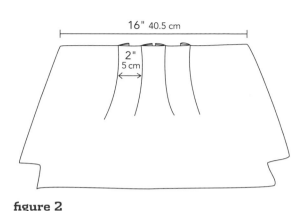

figure 2

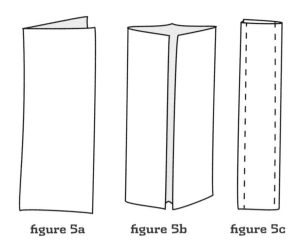

figure 5a   figure 5b   figure 5c

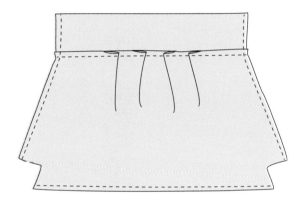

figure 3

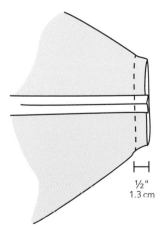

figure 4

fold line and press. Topstitch each long side, ¼" (6 mm) from the folded edges (**figure 5c**).

10 Thread each tab through a 2" (5 cm) rectangle ring, and fold the tab in half. Pin or clip the aligned raw edges of each tab to the top raw edge of the right side of bag exterior 3" (7.5 cm) from each side seam (**figure 6**); stitch with a ½" (1.3 cm) seam allowance.

ASSEMBLE THE LINING

11 Repeat Steps 2, 3 and 4 to mark and sew the pleats in the Lining pieces.

12 With right sides together, stitch one faux leather facing piece to the pleated edge of each Lining piece with a ½" (1.3 cm) seam allowance. Using a press cloth, press the seam allowance toward the facing, and topstitch the facing ¼" (6 mm) from the seam.

13 Repeat Step 7 to sew the side seams, leaving an 8" (20.5 cm) opening in the center of the bottom seam for turning the bag. Press seams open.

14 Repeat Step 8 to sew the corners.

COMPLETE THE BAG

15 With the faux leather bag right side out and the lining wrong side out, place the Lining over the exterior (right sides together) with the top raw edges of both pieces and side seams aligned. The exterior will be nested completely within the lining and the tabs will be sandwiched between the two layers. Pin or clip all the layers together. Sew the top raw edge with a ½" (1.3 cm) seam allowance, easing the pieces to fit together so the side seams are aligned.

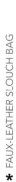

16 Turn the bag right side out, pulling the bag exterior through the opening in the bottom seam of the Lining. Fold the lining to the inside of the bag and press along the top of the bag. Topstitch the top edge of the bag ¼" (6 mm) from the edge. Whipstitch the opening in the lining closed.

17 Repeat Step 9 to fold and stitch each Strap. Trim the ends of the Straps to be sure all layers are even.

18 Thread each end of one Strap through the rings on one side of the bag and bring the ends of the Strap together to meet in the center, forming a loop. Flatten the loop so that the two layers of Straps are aligned with each other and the raw ends are butted together in the center. Clip the four layers together, and stitch along the existing topstitching 2" (5 cm) on either side of the spot where the raw ends of the Strap meet through all the layers to reinforce the Strap join. Repeat with the second strap on the other side of the bag. (*Optional:* to further secure the raw ends of the Strap, edgestitch each end.)

19 Following the manufacturer's instructions, install one stud on the front of each Tab and on each end of each Strap 1½" (3.8 cm) from the folded edge.

RESOURCES
Brett recommends:

Tandy Leather Supplies for metal rivets with screw-in studs (tandyleatherfactory.com).

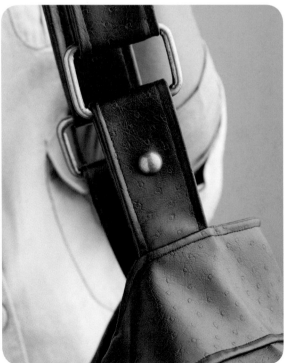

TIPS FOR SEWING WITH
faux leather

Coined from a combination of the words "plastic" and "leather," pleather came on the scene in the 1970s. Some pleathers are made to mimic their on-the-hoof counterparts, with embossed patterning for crocodile, cheetah, snakeskin, and so forth. Others are made to be totally mod, in bright, shiny finishes and bold fashion colors.

Pleather is made from polyester, polyurethane, polyvinyl chloride (PVC) or a combination of these synthetic fibers. It's lighter than leather, easier to care for, and less expensive. Some pleathers can be handwashed and others simply wiped clean with a damp cloth.

This fun fabric usually has a knit or woven backing for easier sewing and to add a bit of stretch to the finished garment. Pleather is available in many weights, from lightweight and supple animal-skin patterning to heavier-grained upholstery weights. The big advantage: there's no worry about cutting between holes or matching hides when the fabric comes by the yard.

To make sewing easier, choose a pattern with simple lines and few construction details. Avoid darts if possible. And it's best to purchase a little extra fabric on which to practice stitching before you begin sewing your project.

SEAMING

Use clips to hold layers in place for sewing, or use a light application of glue stick, but only within the seam allowances (**figure 1**).

Sew with a Teflon foot to keep the fabric moving evenly. This is especially important when you sew on the right side of pleather. If you don't have a Teflon foot, place tissue paper or tear-away stabilizer along the stitching line.

Use a longer than normal stitch length because small stitches may perforate the pleather and weaken the seam. A small (9/65) Microtex (sharp) needle will help minimize visible needle holes. If you're sewing on heavy pleather, increase the needle size.

Topstitching seams with a long stitch (3.5 mm) helps to hold them in place. Seam allowances can be opened or turned to one side, and topstitching can be done with a straight or zigzag, depending on the desired look (see **figures 2, 3, and 4**).

CUTTING

When you cut a project from pleather, cut a single layer at a time. If you must cut a double thickness, fold the fabric wrong sides together to avoid having the layers stick together. Cut projects using a "with nap" layout to avoid shading concerns and place pins only within the seam allowances — pin holes are permanent! Better yet, use weights for cutting.

PRESSING

Depending on the fiber content, pressing strategies vary, but don't ever press PVC pleather or it will simply melt. The knit backing on the wrong side can be pressed with a cool iron and press cloth. If you need to tame seams, use a clapper or wooden iron stick to "press" seams open or to one side.

HEMMING AND CLOSURES

Hemming can be done by hand, catching the knit backing only, or hems can be machine topstitched. For closures, think about zippers or hook-and-loop tape, depending on the project styling. Basting tape works well to hold zippers in place for stitching. If you choose to use snaps, reinforce the area with interfacing before inserting them.

1. Clamped seam ready for stitching

2. Single top-stitched seam

3. Double topstitched seam

4. Zigzag topstitched seam

5. In-seam buttonhole

Make a checkbook cover that will help a friend organize everything she needs—cash, cards, checkbook, and a pen—all in one handy organizer. Combine scraps of pretty prints from your stash for a designer-look accessory. *by* AYUMI TAKAHASHI

charming CHECKBOOK COVER

FABRIC

—8" × 7¾" (20.5 × 19.5 cm) scrap of print cotton for Cover Shell

—9" × 18" (23 × 45.5 cm) scrap of linen for Cover Lining (*shown:* natural)

—8" × 6¼" (20.5 × 16 cm) scrap of print cotton for Checkbook Pocket

—Three 8" × 4" (20.5 × 10 cm) scraps of assorted print cottons for Card Pockets

—2¼" × 45" (5.5 × 114.5 cm) strip OR ⅛ yd (11.5cm) of 45" (114.5 cm) wide print cotton for binding tape

—One print cotton scrap, at least 2" × 2" (5 × 5 cm) to cover button

OTHER SUPPLIES

—¼ yd (23 cm) of double-sided heavyweight fusible interfacing

—⅛ yd (11.5 cm) of light- to medium-weight fusible interfacing

—Cotton sewing thread to match or coordinate with Card Pockets fabric

—Cotton sewing thread to match binding tape

—One ⅛" (3 mm) coverable button with covering kit

—9¾" (25 cm) of faux-leather cord

—Chalk pen

FINISHED SIZE

—3⅝" × 8" (9.3 × 20.5 cm) closed; 7¾" × 8" (19.5 × 20.5 cm) open

NOTES

—All seam allowances are ¼" (6 mm) unless otherwise noted.

CUT THE FABRIC

1 Cut the following pieces as directed (label each piece to avoid confusion):

From the linen, cut:

— One 8" × 7¾" (20.5 × 19.5 cm) piece for Lining

— One 8" × 7¼" (20.5 × 18.5 cm) piece for Upper Pocket

— One 2" × 3¼" (5 × 8.5 cm) piece for Pen Holder

From the binding fabric (if using yardage) cut:

— One 2¼" (5.5 cm) × width of fabric strip for binding tape

From the light- to medium-weight interfacing, cut:

— One 8" × 3⅛" (20.5 × 8 cm) piece

From the heavyweight interfacing, cut:

— One 8" × 7¾" (20.5 × 19.5 cm) piece

ASSEMBLE THE CHECKBOOK COVER

2 Fold each Card Pocket piece in half lengthwise, with right sides together. Sew the long edges together on each and then turn right side out through one of the open short ends; press.

3 Pin one prepared Card Pocket piece onto the linen Upper Pocket, right sides up and with the top folded edge of the Card Pocket 1" (2.5 cm) down from the top long edge of the Upper Pocket piece. Edgestitch the bottom (seamed) edge of the Card Pocket to secure it to the Upper Pocket piece.

4 Pin another Card Pocket piece on top of the Upper Pocket piece, placing its top edge ½" (1.3 cm) down from the top edge of the previous Card Pocket. Edgestitch the bottom edge. Repeat the entire step to attach the remaining Card Pocket piece.

5 Use a ruler and a chalk pen to draw a line in the center of these three pockets (4" [10 cm] from either side). Topstitch through all layers along this line, backtacking at the ends and sewing over the line of stitching a second time to reinforce it.

6 Fold the Upper Pocket piece in half lengthwise with wrong sides together and press. Place this piece right side up on the Lining piece, aligning the raw top edges

of the Upper Pocket piece with the long top edge of the Lining piece. Baste ⅛" (3 mm) from the side and top edges of the pocket piece to attach it to the Lining, leaving the bottom edge open.

7 Fold the Checkbook Pocket piece in half lengthwise with wrong sides together. Insert the light- to medium-weight interfacing piece between the layers and fuse it in place following the manufacturer's instructions. Pin the fused checkbook pocket right side up on top of the Lining piece with the pocket's bottom raw edges aligned with the bottom edge of the Lining piece (opposite the Upper Pocket piece). Baste ⅛" (3 mm) from the side and bottom edges of the checkbook pocket to attach it to the Lining, leaving the top folded edge open.

8 Create a pen holder as follows. Fold ¼" (6 mm) under along one short edge of the Pen Holder piece and topstitch about 3/16" (5 mm) from the folded edge to the hem. Press under ¼" (6 mm) along both long edges. Pin the Pen Holder to the Lining, aligning the left raw edges so the holder will open to the right and butting the top folded edge of the Pen Holder up to the lowest card pocket. (Make sure these pieces are not overlapping.) Edgestitch this folded-under long edge of the Pen Holder to secure it to the Lining. Butt the remaining long edge of the Pen Holder against the checkbook pocket, allowing the excess Pen Holder fabric to bunch up. Edgestitch the folded-under edge to secure it to the Lining, being sure to keep the excess fabric out of the way of the stitching. Fold the excess Pen Holder fabric into a tuck in the middle of the short raw edge and baste ⅛" (3 mm) from the edge to hold the tuck in place on the lining.

9 Following the manufacturer's instructions, fuse the heavyweight interfacing piece to the wrong side of the Cover Shell. Follow the manufacturer's instructions to cover the button with the 2" × 2" (5 × 5 cm) fabric scrap, then handsew the covered button 1" (2.5 cm) from the bottom long edge and 4" (10 cm) from either short edge.

10 Fold the faux-leather cord into a loop and center the ends on the edge of the Cover Shell opposite the button. Baste the ends in place ⅛" (3 mm) from the edge of the Cover Shell.

11 Fuse the assembled lining to the remaining side of the heavyweight interfacing, positioning the card

> ✚ Use a quarter-inch presser foot for perfect ¼" (6 mm) seam allowances. Use a quilting guide attachment whenever you're quilting layers of fabric for a bag, and always use a needle that's appropriate for the fabric you're working with. —AYUMI TAKAHASHI

pockets over the button side of the shell and the checkbook pocket over the cord side of the shell.

12 Fold under one short edge of the binding tape piece by ¼" (6 mm) and press. Create double layer binding according to the instructions on page 129, and bind the raw edges following the instructions for Binding with Mitered Corners, catching the basted end of the cord in the binding seam but leaving the loop end loose.

13 Knot the cord about ¾" (2 cm) from the end of the loop so it can fit over the button and hold it securely.

Cool styling combined with clever design make this unique gusseted asymmetrical bag equally fun to make and wear. With the extended strap across your body, it serves as a messenger bag; if you use the bound cutout handle, it becomes a stylish shoulder bag. *by* STEFFANI K. BURTON

drop-top
MESSENGER BAG

FABRIC
—1¼ yd (1.1 m) of 54" (137 cm) wide wool fabric for shell and tabs (Main)
—1 yd (91.5 cm) of 54" (137 cm) wide home-decorator-weight cotton for lining and interior cell pocket (Contrast)
—Twelve assorted accent scraps, about 5" × 10" (12.5 × 25.5 cm) for bars (*shown:* assorted wool scraps)
—18" × 18" (45.5 × 45.5 cm) fabric square to use for armhole bias binding

OTHER SUPPLIES
—2½ yd (2.3 m) of 23" (58.5 cm) wide lightweight woven fusible interfacing (*shown:* Bosal 300)

—Press cloth
—Matching sewing thread
—1⅔ yd (1.5 m) of 3¾" (9.5 cm) wide jute upholstery webbing
—Size 100/16 jeans sewing machine needle
—Two 1" (2.5 cm) heavy-duty swivel clips
—Two 1" (2.5 cm) D rings
—1¾" (4.5 cm) buckle (*shown:* hammered silver oval buckle)
—Drop-Top Messenger Bag pattern on Pattern Insert

FINISHED SIZE
About 15" wide × 20" tall × 3½" deep at the gusseted bottom (38 × 51 × 9 cm). When folded over and using the long strap, height is 11" (28 cm) not including strap. Including

adjustable strap, total height is adjustable from about 25–37" (63.5–94 cm).

NOTES
—All seam allowances are ½" (1.3 cm) unless otherwise noted.
—Take care when pressing and fusing interfacing to the wool. Use a press cloth and make sure the iron is set to the appropriate temperature to avoid shrinkage.
—Jute webbing can be found at upholstery businesses or your local fabric/craft store.
—The buckle used for the sample bag was removed from a belt, but similar buckles can be found at fabric/craft stores or online.

—The term "subcut" in the instructions simply refers to cutting pieces you have already cut into smaller pieces.

CUT THE FABRIC

1 Cut the following pieces as directed, transferring all pattern markings to the wrong side of the fabric. Note that the shell Main Panels will not be cut until later.

From Main fabric:

—One Gusset

—Two strips, 4½" (11.5 cm) wide × wof (width of fabric); subcut the following rectangles from these strips for accent strip ends:

—Twelve rectangles, 1¾" × 4½" (4.5 × 11.5 cm)

—Twelve rectangles, 2" × 4½" (5 × 11.5 cm)

—Eight rectangles, 2¼" × 4½" (5.5 × 11.5 cm)

—Twelve rectangles, 2½" × 4½" (6.5 × 11.5 cm)

—Four rectangles, 3½" wide × 14" tall (9 × 35.5 cm) for Side Extensions

—Two rectangles, 3" tall × 18½" wide (7.5 × 47 cm) for Bottom Extensions

—Two rectangles, 12" tall × 18½" wide (30.5 × 47 cm) for Top Extensions

—One rectangle 4" × 7" (10 × 18 cm) for Tabs

From Contrast fabric:

—Two Main Panels (cut 1, cut 1 reverse); transfer cell pocket placement dots to the right side of one Panel

—One Gusset

—One 4½" wide × 11" long (11.5 × 28 cm) rectangle for Cell Pocket

From lightweight woven fusible interfacing:

—Four Main Panels (cut 2, cut 2 reverse)

—Two Gussets

—One 3½" × 6½" (9 × 16.5 cm) rectangle for Tabs

From assorted accent scraps:

Cut two of each of the following rectangles for accent bars:

—1½" × 6" (3.8 × 15 cm)

—1¾" × 7¾" (4.5 × 19.5 cm)

—1¾" × 8½" (4.5 × 21.5 cm)

—1¾" × 10" (4.5 × 25.5 cm)

—2" × 7¾" (5 × 19.5 cm)

—2" × 8" (5 × 20.5 cm)

—2" × 8½" (5 × 21.5 cm)

—2¼" × 6½" (5.5 × 16.5 cm)

—2¼" × 7" (5.5 × 18 cm)

—2½" × 7" (6.5 × 18 cm)

—2½" × 8" (6.5 × 20.5 cm)

—2½" × 8½" (6.5 × 21.5 cm)

From armhole binding fabric:

—Two bias strips, 2" wide × 22" long (5 × 56 cm)

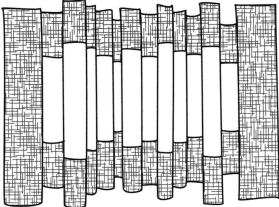

figure 1

MAKE THE TABS

2 Fuse the interfacing Tabs piece, centered, to the wrong side of the Main fabric Tabs piece, following the manufacturer's instructions.

3 Fold the Tabs piece in half lengthwise, wrong sides together, and press. Open and press the long raw edges toward the center crease so that they meet at the crease. Refold the piece in along the center crease, enclosing the raw edges. Press. The piece should now measure 1" × 7" (2.5 × 18 cm). Edgestitch down both long edges. Cut this strip in half widthwise so you have two 1" × 3½" (2.5 × 9 cm) Tab pieces. Loop one completed Tab through one D ring and baste the raw ends together. Repeat the entire step with the second Tab and D ring. Set both aside.

SEW THE STRIP SETS

4 Matching widths, sew an accent strip rectangle of Main fabric to each short end of all accent bar rectangles (for example, a 1¾" × 4½" [4.5 × 11.5 cm] Main fabric piece will be joined to each short end of one 1¾" × 7¾" [4.5 × 19.5 cm] accent bar). Assembled pieces will vary in length. Press all seam allowances open.

5 Separate your pieced strips into two stacks, each containing one of each size you stitched. You will be creating two strip sets, one for each side of your bag shell.

6 Lay out one stack of pieced strips in a pleasing manner, staggering the accent bars. Once you have an arrangement you like, sew the long edges of adjacent strips together and press seam allowances open (**figure 1**, viewed from right side).

7 Center one 3½" × 14" (9 × 35.5 cm) Main fabric Side Extension rectangle on each short end of your strip set. Pin with right sides together and stitch into place (**figure 1**). Press seam allowances open.

8 Repeat Steps 6 and 7 with the remaining stack of strips. Trim each strip set to 11" tall × 18½" wide (28 × 47 cm).

CONSTRUCT THE PIECED SHELL MAIN PANELS

9 Sew a Top and Bottom Extension rectangle to each of the trimmed strip sets with right sides together, along the 18½" (47 cm) sides. Press the seam allowances toward the Extension pieces.

10 Using the Main Panel pattern piece, cut two Main Panels (cut one, cut one reverse) from the pieced strip sets. Be sure to center the pattern and align the marked guidelines (from the pattern) with the strip set seams. Remember to transfer all pattern markings to the wrong side (do not transfer cell pocket markings).

11 Fuse the interfacing Main Panel pieces to the wrong sides of the just-cut Main Panels, making sure the seam allowances remain pressed as directed in Step 9.

12 If desired, topstitch ⅛" (3 mm) inside and ⅛" (3 mm) outside all edges of each accent bar piece.

CONSTRUCT THE SHELL BAG

13 Fuse the interfacing Gusset to the wrong side of the Main fabric Gusset.

14 Aligning the center bottom notches, pin one Main Panel to the Gusset, right sides together, pinning around the bottom curved edge. Sew the pieces together, starting and stopping ½" (1.3 cm) before the ends of the Gusset piece.

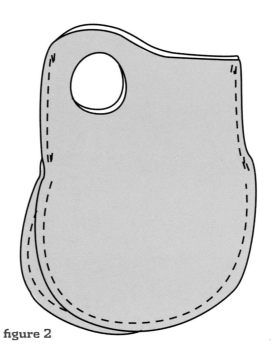

figure 2

15 Using the Tab placement notches, align the raw edges of the tabs with the raw edges of the Main Panel so that your D rings face in. Baste the Tabs onto the shell Main Panel.

16 Attach the remaining Main Panel to the other side of the Gusset as in Step 14.

17 Continue sewing up both sides of the Main Panels and backtack at each end (**figure 2**). Press the seam allowances open and then turn the bag right side out.

MAKE THE CELL POCKET + CONSTRUCT THE LINING

18 Fold the Cell Pocket piece in half, right sides together, so it measures 5½" × 4½" (14 × 11.5 cm). Using ¼" (6 mm) seam allowances, sew all raw edges, leaving a 2½" (6.5 cm) gap for turning on one side. Clip the corners and turn right side out. Press flat, turning the seam allowances in at the gap.

19 Topstitch across the folded top edge of the pocket, ³⁄₁₆" (5 mm) from the edge.

20 Using the pocket placement dots on the Contrast fabric Main Panel as a guide, pin the pocket in place on the right side of one Main Panel. Edgestitch the pocket in place around the three seamed edges, leaving the top folded edge unstitched and closing the gap that remains in the pocket side.

21 Repeat Steps 13–17, excluding Step 15, to construct the lining bag. Press all seam allowances open.

ASSEMBLE THE BAG

22 With the shell bag turned right side out, place it inside the lining bag, aligning the top edges. Pin and then sew the top edges together.

23 Clip the curves and side seam "V." Press the seam allowances open.

24 Turn the bag right side out through the armhole, press, and topstitch around the top of your bag ⅛" (3 mm) from the edge.

FINISHING

25 Baste the shell and lining together ¼" (6 mm) from the edge around the armhole on the front and back panels of the bag.

26 Refer to Create Binding on page 129 to prepare the binding strips for use as double-fold binding. Open the binding and press ½" (1.3 cm) to the wrong side at one short end of each strip. Starting with the folded-under end of the binding, pin one binding strip to each lining armhole, matching the raw edges. Leaving about 2" (5 cm) of the binding fabric free at the beginning, sew the binding to the armhole along the first crease. When you are a few inches from the beginning edge of the binding fabric, stop sewing, overlap the pressed beginning edge of the binding by ½" (1.3 cm), and trim the working edge to fit. Finish sewing the binding. Refold the binding along all creases and then fold it over the armhole raw edges to the shell side, enclosing the raw edges. The folded edge of the binding should just cover the stitches visible on the shell. Edgestitch the binding to the shell through all layers (or slipstitch in place by hand if you prefer).

27 Fold the jute webbing in half lengthwise and press. Topstitch ¼" (6 mm) from both long edges. This is your strap.

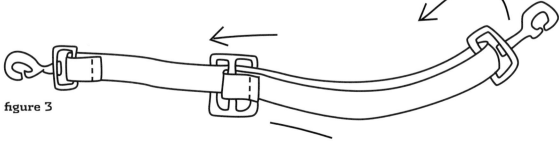

figure 3

28 Secure one end of the strap to your buckle by folding 2" (5 cm) of the strap over the buckle's center bar. Sew back and forth across the strap several times near the raw end to trap the center bar.

29 Slide one swivel clip onto the loose end of the strap and run that end of the strap through the buckle (over the already stitched end of the strap attached to the center bar). Secure the second swivel clip to the loose end of the strap by folding over 2" (5 cm) and sewing across the strap as described in Step 28 (**figure 3**).

30 Clip the strap to the D rings on the bag with the swivel clips. To use your bag, wear the shoulder hole over your arm with the bag fully extended or allow both layers of the top of the bag to fold over like a flap and use the jute strap; when folded over, the shoulder hole becomes a new design feature, allowing the accent bars to peek through!

SEWING WITH *wool*

Wool fabrics fall into two categories: woolens and worsteds. Woolens are made from shorter, fuzzier fibers with little twist. Examples include flannels, tweeds, and coatings. Worsteds are constructed of longer, tightly twisted fibers, producing lighter weight fabrics such as gabardine, challis, and crepes. Wool fabrics can also be woven in a variety of patterns, knitted (like jersey), or felted.

Technically, wool comes from a sheep, but the term can also be used to refer to blends of other animal hairs, such as cashmere, alpaca, vicuña, and angora.

Sewing with wool is easy even for beginners, because the fiber is very forgiving and can be easily shaped with steam. Use these helpful hints when sewing your wool projects:

■ Preshrink the fabric before cutting if it isn't labeled "ready for the needle." A simple steaming works well, either at home or by the dry cleaner.

■ Use a "with nap" cutting layout to avoid shading. For very bulky fabrics, cut one layer at a time.

■ Choose an interfacing that is compatible with the fabric weight.

■ Use a universal-point sewing needle in a size suitable for the wool's weight and thread type.

■ Trim and grade seam allowances to reduce bulk.

■ Press seams and other construction details as you sew. Always use steam, and on hard-finish wools such as worsted suitings use a press cloth to prevent shine.

■ Finish seams by serging or pinking, or use a lining to hide seams and help a wool garment keep its shape. Encase seam allowances on loosely woven wools.

types of wool

1. CHALLIS Soft and lightweight, challis is made with worsted yarns and is often printed.

2. CREPE Made with very twisted yarns, crepe has a surface that looks pebbly or crinkly—wrinkles fall away.

3. GABARDINE This firmly woven fabric has a fine twill (diagonal) weave patterning.

4. FLANNEL A slightly napped surface makes this the perfect fabric for classic wardrobe pieces like pants and jackets.

5. JERSEY A knitted wool with purl stitches on one side and knit stitches on the other side, jersey is soft and drapable for unstructured dresses and tops.

6. COATING This heavyweight wool with a dense, napped surface keeps wind and weather at bay when used for outerwear.

7. TWEED Made with flecks of several colors, tweed is popular for sportswear and casual clothing.

Arrive in style with this coordinating set of chic travel accessories that includes a garment bag, a duffel, and a cosmetic bag. The brightly colored prints will liven up your day, even on a red-eye flight! *by* CAROL ZENTGRAF

weekend travel ENSEMBLE

Garment Bag
FABRIC
—2⅞ yd (2.6 m) each of two different 54" (137 cm) wide home decorator fabrics for shell (Main; purchase extra fabric if you want to match the print across the center front zipper; see the sidebar on page 97) and lining (Contrast)

OTHER SUPPLIES
—Coordinating sewing thread
—¼" (6 mm) wide self-adhesive, double-sided basting tape
—48" (122 cm) long two-way zipper or 4' (1.2 m) of zipper-by-the-yard for front
—22" (56 cm) zipper for back pocket
—½" (1.3 cm) wide double-stick fusible web tape
—26" (66 cm) length of ⅜" (1 cm) wide ribbon for tie
—Removable fabric marker
—Hip curve ruler (optional)
—Zipper foot for sewing machine

NOTES
—All seam allowances are ½" (1.3 cm) unless otherwise noted.
—Sew all seams with right sides together.

Duffel Bag
FABRIC
—⅝ yd (57 cm) each of two 54" (137 cm) wide home decorator fabrics for shell (A) and lining (B; see Notes)
—¼ yd (23 cm) of contrasting 54" (137 cm) wide home decorator fabric for pocket and straps (C)

OTHER SUPPLIES
—1 yd (91.5 cm) of 45" (114.5 cm) wide fusible batting/fusible fleece (see Choosing Batting sidebar, page 100)
—Self-adhesive, double-sided basting tape
—19" (48.5 cm) separating zipper
—Coordinating sewing thread
—Spray adhesive
—10" (25.5 cm) length of 1" (2.5 cm)-wide ribbon
—Handsewing needle (optional)
—Duffel Bag template on pattern insert

NOTES
—All seam allowances are ½" (1.3 cm) unless otherwise noted.
—The yardage requirements for fabrics A and B are based on a nondirectional print. If

you are using a directional print, you'll need to allow more fabric to cut the shell and lining rectangles with the print running the same direction as the End Panel.

Cosmetic Bag
FABRIC
—½ yd (45.5 cm) of 54" (137 cm) wide home decorator fabric for shell (Main)
—½ yd (45.5 cm) of lightweight vinyl for lining

OTHER SUPPLIES
—Self-adhesive, double-sided basting tape
—Coordinating sewing thread
—16" (40.5 cm) zipper
—6" (15 cm) length of 1" (2.5 cm) wide ribbon
—Handsewing needle (optional)
—Cosmetic Bag template on pattern insert

NOTES
—Use basting tape instead of pins when working with vinyl; pin marks will be permanent.
—Do not touch a hot iron to the vinyl.

garment bag
CUT THE FABRIC

1 *From the Main fabric, cut:*

—Two 12½" × 50" (31.5 × 127 cm) rectangles for Front Panel

—One 24" × 16" (61 × 40.5 cm) rectangle for back Top Panel

—One 24" × 35" (61 × 89 cm) rectangle for back Bottom Panel

—One 5" × 24" (12.5 × 61 cm) Bottom Strip

—Two 5" × 58" (12.5 × 147.5 cm) Side/Top Strips

—One 5" × 16" (12.5 × 40.5 cm) strip for Handle

From the Contrast fabric, cut:

—Two 12½" × 50" (31.5 × 127 cm) rectangles for Front Panel Lining

—One 24" × 50" (61 × 127 cm) rectangle for Back Panel Lining

—One 5" × 24" (12.5 × 61 cm) Bottom Lining Strip

—Two 5" × 58" (12.5 × 147.5 cm) Side/Top Lining strips

ASSEMBLE THE BAG SHELL

2 Use the pieces cut from Main fabric for Steps 3 and 5–7. Use the pieces cut from Contrast fabric for Steps 4, 8, and 9.

3 Place the Front P anels on a flat surface with right sides together. On the right-hand edge, make a mark 9" (23 cm) from the top. Use a fabric marker and a hip curve to draw a curved line from the 9" (23 cm) mark to the top left corner of the panels, or sketch a curve freehand. Cut through both layers along the

matching the print

When using a patterned fabric, such as a large floral print, you'll need to carefully match the print on adjoining pattern pieces. To do this, you can temporarily place adjoining pieces right sides together (as they would be sewn) and pick an adjoining point at the top and bottom of each piece to check the placement; mark these spots with a pencil. When you are placing each pattern piece in preparation for cutting, make sure you line up your pencil marks along like areas of the print so that the print will be continuous once those pieces are joined (you may need to ensure that the two pattern pieces, once joined, will create one full element of the print, such as a flower). Alternatively, you could use the same process to place a cut piece over an adjoining pattern piece that has not yet been cut, adjusting the placement of the pattern piece until the print matches up with the already-cut piece. Make sure that all adjoining pieces are matched before or as you cut.

marked line. Fold the Back Top Panel in half, right sides together, and use the Front Panels as a pattern to cut the top corners of the Back Top Panel to match the Front Panels.

4 Using the Main Fabric Panels as a pattern, round the upper corners of the corresponding Contrast Lining pieces.

5 Stitch and baste the center front edges of the front panels together, using a regular stitch length for 1" (2.5 cm) at each end of the seam and switching to a long stitch length in between. Press the seam allowances open. Apply the self-adhesive basting tape to the right side of the 48" (122 cm) zipper tapes and remove the tape's paper backing. Apply the zipper, right side down, on the pressed seam allowances, centering the zipper teeth on the seam. From the right side of the fabric, use a zipper foot and stitch the zipper in place ⅜" (1 cm) from the center seam. Remove the basting stitches, leaving the 1" (2.5 cm) seams at the top and bottom intact.

6 Stitch and baste the Back Top and Bottom Panels together, using a regular stitch length for 1" (2.5 cm) at each end of the seam and switching to a long stitch

garment bag

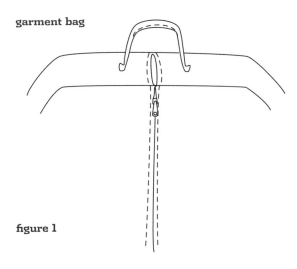

figure 1

garment bag

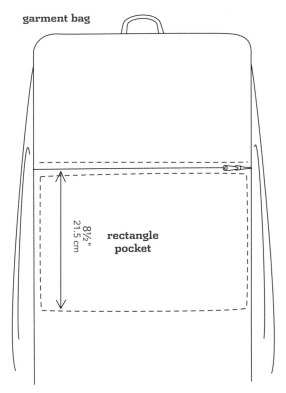

8½"
21.5 cm

**rectangle
pocket**

figure 2

length in between. Repeat Step 5 to apply the 22"
(56 cm) zipper.

7 Sew the Side/Top Strips to each end of the bottom
Strip, beginning and ending the stitching ½" (1.3 cm)
from each end of the seams. Match the center of the
bottom strip to the bag front seam and pin. Match the
seams in the Bottom/Side Strips to the lower corners
of the bag front and pin; the ½" (1.3 cm) left open
at each end of the seams will spread apart to pivot
around the corners. Continue pinning the strip to the
bag front: up the sides, around the curved edges, and
to the center front. Press the excess strip fabric to
the wrong side at each end, but do not trim. Sew the
strips to the bag front as pinned. Repeat to sew the
back to the free side of the strips. Turn the bag right
side out and press.

ASSEMBLE THE LINING

8 Sew the Front Panel Lining pieces together for 1"
(2.5 cm) at each end of the seam. Press ⅝" (1.5 cm)
to the wrong side along the remaining center front
edges and secure with fusible web tape, following the
manufacturer's instructions.

9 Follow Step 7 to assemble the lining front, back,
and sides; do not turn right side out.

FINISH BAG

10 Place the lining inside the bag shell, wrong sides
together, aligning the seams and the pressed ends of
the Side/Top Strips. The lining's center front edges

should be ⅛" (3 mm) away from the zipper teeth. Pin
the lining to the shell along the zipper opening and
the pressed edges in the Side/Top Strips. Sew the
pressed edges of the shell and lining Side/Top Strips
together on each side of the center front, sewing ⅛"
(3 mm) from the pressed edges through all layers,
creating an opening for hangers (see **figure 1**). Stitch
over the previous lines of stitching on each side of the
zipper through all thicknesses to join the layers along
the zipper opening.

11 On the bag back, measure and mark a line across
the lower back panel 8½" (21.5 cm) below the zipper
teeth. To sew the back shell to the lining and create
the back pocket, open the front zipper and move the
front panels out of the way. Pin the shell and lining
together just above the zipper, along the side seams,
and below the guideline. From the back shell side,
stitch through the shell and lining layers along the top
zipper stitching line, the side seams, and the guideline
below the zipper to form a rectangular pocket with
the zipper at the top (**figure 2**). Do not stitch through
the front panels.

MAKE THE HANDLE

12 Press ½" (1.3 cm) to the wrong side on each short end of the Handle strip and use fusible web tape to secure. Press the strip in half lengthwise with wrong sides together. Open the strip and press the long edges to the wrong side to meet at the center fold. Refold along the center crease and press once more. Edgestitch both long edges.

13 Measure and mark the shell side/top strip 3½" (9 cm) on each side of the center opening. Center the Handle ends on the Side/Top Strip, placing the fused ends on the marks. Make sure the shell and lining are properly aligned, then sew the Handle ends to the bag (**figure 2**), stitching across the Handle close to the end and again ½" (1.3 cm) from the first stitching.

14 With the garment bag unzipped, measure and mark the center of the Bottom Strip. Make sure the lining and shell are matched correctly and pin on either side of the mark. Fold the ribbon in half, widthwise, to find its center. Match the ribbon center to the center of the Bottom Strip and sew across the ribbon to attach it to the bag. Be careful to catch only the ribbon and the center of the Bottom Strip (shell and lining) in the stitches. Tie in a bow to use the bag full-length. To carry the bag folded up, tie the ribbon around the hangers at the top of the bag.

+ I like to cut a bag lining from a thrift-store pillowcase in a pattern or color that coordinates with the bag's outside fabric. I often find a pillowcase at my local thrift store for less than a dollar that will provide enough fabric for lining and even for an inside pocket. I avoid black, as it can make bag contents hard to see, and white, because it's hard to keep clean. **—BLAIR STOCKER**

duffel bag
CUT THE FABRIC

1 Trace and cut out the End Panel and Pocket patterns from the Pattern Insert.

From fabric A, cut:

—Two End Panels, using the pattern

—One 35" × 20" (89 × 51 cm) rectangle for Bag Shell

From fabric B, cut:

—Two End Panels, using the pattern

—One 35" × 20" (89 × 51 cm) rectangle for bag Lining

From fabric C, cut:

—One Pocket, using the pattern

—Two 4" × 25" (10 × 63.5 cm) strips for Handles

From the fusible batting, cut:

—Two End Panels, using the pattern

—One 35" × 20" (89 × 51 cm) rectangle for bag

ASSEMBLE THE BAG

2 Following the manufacturer's instructions, fuse the batting to the wrong side of the corresponding shell (A) pieces: two End Panels and one body rectangle.

3 Press ½" (1.3 cm) to the wrong side along both 20" (51 cm) edges of the Bag Shell and Lining rectangles. Apply basting tape to the pressed-under edges on both fabrics. Separate the zipper halves. With the shell fabric and zipper halves right side up, remove the paper backing from the basting tape and adhere a

duffel bag

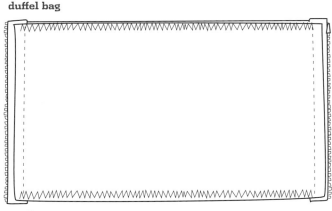

figure 3

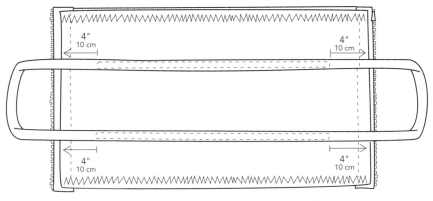

figure 4

zipper tape to each end of the Bag Shell rectangle, positioning the Shell so the zipper teeth remain exposed. Repeat to adhere the Lining rectangle to the wrong side of the zipper tape, making sure the pressed edges of the Bag Shell and Lining are aligned. Topstitch ¼" (6 mm) from the folded edges on both sides of the zipper, catching all layers in the stitches. Serge or zigzag stitch the long edges of the Bag Shell and Lining rectangles together (**figure 3**).

4 Press the Pocket top edge to the wrong side on the line indicated on the pattern. Topstitch ½" (1.3 cm) from the fold. Pin the pocket, right side up, on the right side of one shell fabric End Panel (with batting attached), aligning the side and lower (wider) edges. Using spray adhesive, adhere the wrong side of a lining fabric End Panel to each batting End Panel (only one End Panel has a Pocket) so the batting is sandwiched between the shell and lining pieces. Serge or zigzag stitch the outer edges together as in Step 7.

5 To make the handles, sew the short ends of the handle pieces right sides together to create a continuous loop, making sure the fabric is not twisted. Press the strip in half lengthwise with wrong sides together. Open the fold and press both long edges to the wrong side to meet at the center crease. Refold along the center crease, enclosing the raw edges, and press once again. Edgestitch both long edges.

6 Place the bag rectangle on a flat surface with the shell fabric facing up. Measure and mark a line 4" (10 cm) from each long edge and position basting tape along the lines, beginning and ending 4" (10 cm) from the zipper tapes. Measure to locate the center of the rectangle, midway between the zipper tapes, and mark with a pin on each piece of basting tape; this is the bottom of the bag. Remove the protective paper from the basting tape. Position a seam between the handle sections at the bag bottom on each basting tape and smooth the handle loop into place across the duffle rectangle (see **figure 4**).

7 Beginning at the bag bottom on one side of the handle loop, edgestitch the handle loop to the bag. Sew from the bag bottom to the end of the basting tape, 4" (10 cm) below the zipper; pivot and sew across the handle fabric; pivot again and stitch along the opposite side of the handle. Keep sewing past the bag bottom to the point 4" (10 cm) below the other zipper tape, then pivot as before and return to the starting point. Repeat to sew the other side of the Handle loop to the bag (**figure 4**).

8 Mark the center top of each assembled End Panel. Cut the ribbon in half and make a loop with each half, bringing the short ends together so that one end lies directly on top of the other. Place one loop on the shell side of each End Panel, at the center mark and with the raw edges matched, so that the loop lies on top of the panel. Baste each loop in place ¼" (6 mm) from the edge.

9 Zip the zipper, bringing the short ends of the bag rectangle together. Sew across both ends of the zipper tape just beyond the teeth with a wide, short zigzag stitch or several hand whipstitches. Open the zipper halfway.

10 With fabric sides together, sew the End Panels to the long edges of the bag rectangle, aligning the zipper ends with the center top of each end panel. Clip the rectangle seam allowance at each corner, allowing the seam allowance to spread apart when turning the corners. Turn the bag right side out through the zipper.

choosing batting

Fusible batting, also called fusible fleece, is a firm but thin batting with a permanent adhesive on one side. It's ideal for craft projects like this duffel bag, and bonds the batting to the fabric without stitching.

If fusible batting isn't available, or if you prefer a softer hand, choose regular batting and a spray adhesive instead. Because the spray adhesive creates a temporary bond, batting applied with the spray must also be stitched to the fabric for a permanent bond. Check the batting label for the recommended minimum quilting distance, and sew a grid of lines to hold the shell fabric and batting together before assembling the project.

cosmetic bag
CUT THE FABRIC

1 Trace and cut out the End Panel pattern.

From the Main fabric, cut:

—Two End Panels, using the pattern

—One 12½" × 22" (31.5 × 56 cm) rectangle

From the vinyl, cut:

—Two End Panels, using the pattern

—One 12½" × 22" (31.5 × 56cm) rectangle

ASSEMBLE THE BAG

2 Using basting tape along the edges, adhere the vinyl pieces to the wrong sides of the corresponding fabric pieces.

3 With right sides together, sew the End Panels to the 22" (56 cm) edges of the rectangle, using a ¼" (6 mm) seam allowance. Clip the rectangle's seam allowances as necessary to pivot at the corners, but be careful not to cut through the seam line. Trim the rectangle's upper edges to match the End Panels. Trim the seam allowances to ⅛" (3 mm).

4 Turn the bag right side out. Fold the rectangle and one End Panel, vinyl sides together, along one side seam and topstitch ¼" (6 mm) from the seam through all layers, encasing the seam allowances (see photo above). Repeat to topstitch the seam on the other side of the End Panel. Fold the rectangle and End Panel along the bottom seam and topstitch as before. Repeat to topstitch the seam lines around the second End Panel.

5 On the upper edge of the bag, finger-press ½" (1.3 cm) to the wrong side and secure with basting tape. Topstitch the hem in place ¼" (6 mm) from the bag's upper edge.

6 Trim the zipper to 13" (33 cm) long and stitch across the cut end to secure, using a wide, short zigzag stitch or several hand whipstitches. Unzip the zipper to 1" (2.5 cm) from the bottom. Place the zipper tapes inside the upper edges of the bag sides with the hemmed bag edges ⅛" (3 mm) from the zipper teeth. The zipper will not be sewn to the End Panels; 1" (2.5 cm) at the bottom of the zipper (the portion still zipped) extends beyond the side seams on one end, and the top of the zipper teeth meet the side seams at the other end. Edgestitch along the folded edges of the bag to secure the zipper tapes in place. Fold the excess tape at the top of the zipper down, into the bag, and tack the ends in place as shown in **figure 5**.

7 Press ½" (1.3 cm) to the wrong side on the ribbon ends and fold the ribbon in half to form a loop, with one pressed end lying directly on top of the other. At the bottom of the zipper, tuck the cut end of the zipper tapes between the ribbon layers to hide the zipper tape, then topstitch across the loop, through all layers, securing the loop around the zipper tapes.

+ Use an unexpected fabric, such as a bright pattern or a shiny satin, as a bag lining. That way, even if the exterior of the bag is neutral, there's always something fun going on inside. —BRETT BARA

cosmetic bag

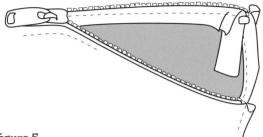

figure 5

Sleek and slim, this side-slung bag features a large angled outer pocket to showcase a contrasting fabric and a curved upper edge for easy carrying. A zipper closure and a roomy interior pocket keep all your essentials safely inside and stylishly organized.

by **MISSY SHEPLER**

side-slung
HANDBAG

FABRIC
—1 yd (91.5 cm) of 45" (114.5 cm) wide cotton fabric for outer bag and strap (Main fabric)

—1 yd (91.5 cm) of 45" (114.5 cm) wide cotton fabric for angled pocket and bag lining (Contrast fabric)

OTHER SUPPLIES
—1¼ yd (114.5 cm) of heavyweight stabilizer such as Pellon® Peltex® 70 Ultra Firm Stabilizer

—⅜ yd (34.5 cm) of light- or medium-weight fusible stabilizer such as Pellon® 808 Craft-Fuse™

—One 9" (23 cm) all-purpose zipper

—Coordinating sewing thread

—Rotary cutter, rigid acrylic ruler, and self-healing mat

—Handsewing needle

—Side-Slung Bag templates on pattern insert.

FINISHED SIZE
10" × 16" × 3" (25.5 × 40.5 × 7.5 cm), excluding strap

NOTES
—All seam allowances are ½" (1.3 cm) unless otherwise indicated.

CUT AND PREPARE THE FABRIC

1 Cut the following pieces as directed.

From the Main fabric:

—One Front/Back and one reversed

—One Long Side Panel

—One Short Side Panel

—Two Zipper Side Panels 1¾" × 10" (4.5 × 25.5 cm)

—Two strips 2½" (6.5 cm) × length of fabric. From these strips, subcut:

—Two Straps 2½" × 27" (6.5 × 68.5 cm)

—One Zipper Start Panel 2½" × 7" (6.5 × 18 cm)

—One Zipper Stop Panel 2½" × 2½" (6.5 × 6.5 cm)

From the Contrast fabric:

—One Outer Pocket and one reversed

—One Front/Back Panel and one reversed

—One Long Side Panel

—One Short Side Panel

—One Lining Pocket 11" × 16¼" (28 × 41.5 cm)

—One Zipper Start Panel 2½" × 7" (6.5 × 18 cm)

—One Zipper Stop Panel 2½" × 2½" (6.5 × 6.5 cm)

—Two Zipper Side Panels 1¾" × 10" (4.5 × 25.5 cm)

—One Strap Cuff 4½" × 6" (11.5 × 15 cm)

From the heavyweight stabilizer:

—One Front/Back Panel and one in reverse

—One Long Side Panel

—One Short Side Panel

From the light- or medium-weight stabilizer:

—Two Zipper Side Panels 1¾" × 10" (4.5 × 25.5 cm)

—One Outer Pocket

PREPARE THE ZIPPER PANEL

2 Place one lining/Contrast fabric Zipper Side Panel right side up, and align the zipper tape, right side up, along one long raw edge. Pin the zipper in place. Place one lightweight stabilizer Zipper Side Panel against the wrong side of one Main fabric Zipper Side Panel, then place the Main fabric Zipper Side Panel right side down on top of the zipper. Align the long raw edges and pin in place.

3 Using a zipper foot, stitch the zipper in place with a scant ⅜" (1 cm) seam allowance (**figure 1**). Fold back the lining, outer/Main fabric, and stabilizer so that the wrong sides of the fabrics are facing with the

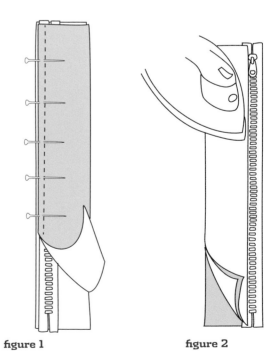

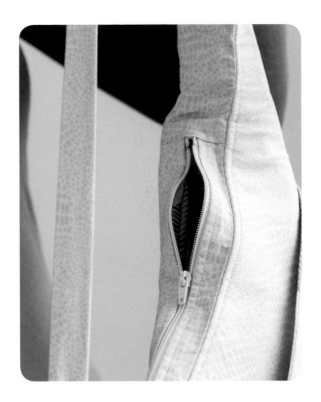

figure 1   **figure 2**

6 Edgestitch around the perimeter of the zipper to secure the pressed edges in place. Trim the Zipper Side Panels even with the Start and Stop Panel edges (**figure 4**).

ASSEMBLE THE OUTER BAG

7 Place the Outer Pocket fabric pieces right sides together; place the Outer Pocket stabilizer piece against the wrong side of the top piece. Align all raw edges and pin in place. Stitch the long angled edge with a ½" (1.3 cm) seam allowance. Flip one pocket piece over the seam, so that the wrong sides of the pocket pieces are together with the stabilizer in between. Press the seam flat and edgestitch along the sewn edge.

8 Place the Outer Pocket on the right side of one Main fabric Front/Back Panel piece, aligning side and bottom raw edges. Using a ¼" (6 mm) seam allowance, sew the pocket to the panel along the side and bottom edges. (*Note:* This is now the bag Front.)

9 Place one Front/Back Panel heavyweight stabilizer piece against the wrong side of the Front. Using a ¼" (6 mm) seam allowance, stitch the stabilizer to the Front around all raw edges.

10 Repeat Step 9 with the Main fabric and stabilizer pieces for the Back Panel, Short Side Panel and Long Side Panel.

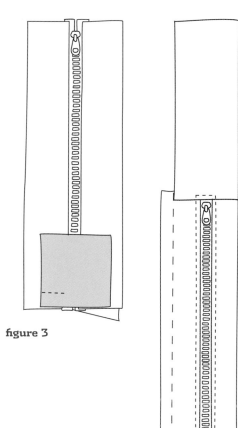

figure 3

figure 4

cut

stabilizer in between. The stitched zipper tape should be enclosed. Press the stitched edge (**figure 2**).

4 Repeat Steps 2 and 3 with the remaining Zipper Side Panels to finish the opposite zipper edge.

5 With right sides together, center the outer/Main fabric Zipper Stop Panel at the bottom of the zipper, so that the seam line will cover the bottom zipper stop. Fold the lining/Contrast fabric to one side and stitch halfway across the seam, stopping at the side panel seam (**figure 3**). Fold the lining to the opposite side and stitch the remaining half of the seam. Repeat to stitch the lining Zipper Stop Panel to the lining side panels. Press the seam allowances away from the zipper. Join the Zipper Start Panels to the top of the zipper in the same way.

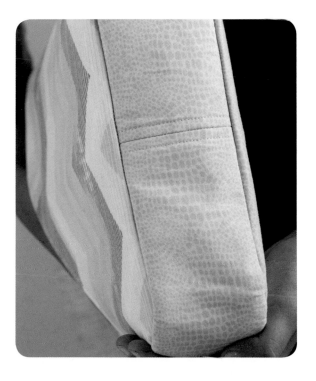

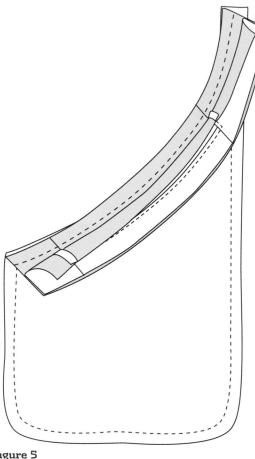

figure 5

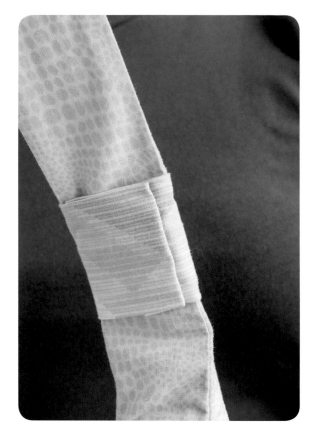

11 With right sides together and the zipper stop nearer the shorter side, align the zipper panel with the upper curved edge of the Front. Making sure not to catch the lining fabric, sew the zipper panel to the Front (unzip the zipper for extra ease when sewing this seam) (**figure 5**). Press the seam toward the Front; edgestitch to secure the pressed edge in place. Repeat this step to sew the Back to the opposite side of the zipper panel.

12 With right sides together, align the wide bottom edges of the Main fabric Short Side Panel and Main fabric Long Side Panel and pin in place. Stitch the two pieces together on the bottom edge with a ½" (1.3 cm) seam allowance, and press the seam open. Topstitch along each side ¼" (6 mm) from the seam (**figure 6**).

13 Open the zipper. With right sides together and matching the Side bottom seam to the center mark indicated on the Front/Back Panel pattern, pin and

sew the Main fabric Side to the Front along the side and bottom edges with a ½" (1.3 cm) seam allowance. Reinforce the seam with a second line of stitching ⅛" (3 mm) inside the seam allowance.

14 Repeat previous step to sew the Side to the Back along the opposite edge. Press the seam allowances toward the bag sides.

ASSEMBLE THE LINING

15 With wrong sides together, fold and press the Lining Pocket in half to make an 11" × 8⅛" (28 × 21 cm) rectangle. Edgestitch ⅛" (3 mm) from the folded edge.

16 Aligning sides and bottom edges, place the Lining Pocket against the right side of one lining Front/Back Panel. Using a ¼" (6 mm) seam, stitch the Lining Pocket in place along the side and bottom edges. Trim the pocket corners to match the curved bag bottom.

17 Repeat Steps 11 through 14 with the Zipper Panel and lining Front, Back, and Side pieces to assemble the bag lining, leaving a 4" (10 cm) section unstitched along one bag side for turning.

18 Turn the bag right side out, pulling the outer bag through the side seam opening in the bag lining. Tucking the seam allowances to the wrong side, hand stitch the side seam opening and the short side seam at the lining zipper stop closed with a whipstitch. Tuck the lining inside the bag. Work the lining into the narrow top of the bag on the bag long side.

ATTACH THE BAG STRAP

19 With right sides together, stitch the two Strap pieces along each long edge using a ¼" (6 mm) seam allowance. Press, then turn the Strap right side out and press again; edgestitch long edges if desired.

20 Align one strap end with the raw edge of the seam allowance at the short side of the outer bag, creating a tuck in the center of the Strap. Stitch the Strap end to the bag side. Stitch again several times within the seam allowance to reinforce the seam.

21 Turn the seam allowance to the wrong side and tuck the secured Strap end inside the outer bag. Fold the seam allowance of the Zipper Stop Panel to the wrong side and hand stitch the panel to the Strap with a slip stitch to secure.

22 Making sure the strap is not twisted, slide the opposite Strap end over the long bag side to cover 1½" (3.8 cm) of the bag side (the bag end will be inside the strap). Boxstitch the Strap end to the bag to secure (**figure 7**).

23 With right sides together, fold the Strap Cuff in half, making a 2¼" × 6" (5.5 × 15 cm) rectangle. Using a ¼" (6 mm) seam allowance, stitch the long sides together. Turn the Cuff right side out. Press and center the seam within the Cuff width.

24 With the seam against the Strap, wrap the Cuff around the box-stitched strap end. Whipstitch one raw edge of the Cuff to the strap. Fold the other raw edge to the wrong side and whipstitch the folded edge to the wrapped Cuff to secure.

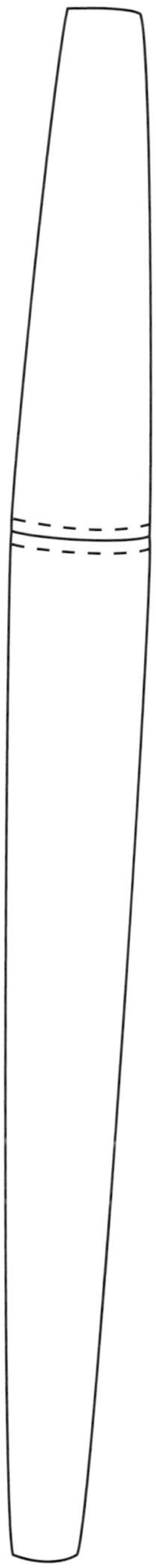

figure 6

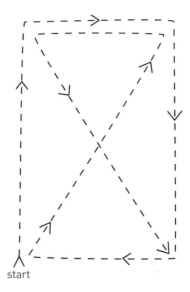

start

figure 7

gadget
MESSENGER BAG

It's easy for laptop bags to get cluttered with cables and connectors. Instead of fumbling through the bag for flash drives, a wireless mouse, and keyboard receivers every time you use your laptop, you can store them plugged into the USB hub built into this bag. Just plug the bag into the computer and get to work! *by* **KEVIN KOSBAB**

FABRIC

—1¾ yd (1.6 m) of 45" (114.5 cm) wide cotton duck canvas for shell and strap (*shown:* light gray)

—¼ yd (23 cm) of 45" (114.5 cm) wide contrasting solid cotton for details (*shown:* orange)

—1 yd (91.5 cm) of 45" (114.5 cm) wide rip-stop nylon for lining (*shown:* gray)

OTHER SUPPLIES

—3 yd (2.7 m) of 20" (51 cm) wide medium-weight fusible interfacing

—9" × 15" (23 × 38 cm) piece of fusible web

—Sewing thread to match shell and contrast fabrics

—6½" (16.5 cm) of ¾" (2 cm) wide sew-in hook-and-loop tape (such as Velcro™)

—Three 2" × ¾" (5 × 2 cm) rectangular rings (see Notes)

—3½ yd (3.2 m) of corded piping to match contrast fabric (two packages of purchased piping, or use filler cord and additional contrast fabric to make your own)

—USB hub with cable (*shown:* 3¾" × 1¼" × ½" [9.5 × 3.2 × 1.3 cm] hub with retractable cable)

—Rotary cutter, rigid acrylic ruler, and self-healing mat

—Fabric marking tool

—Zipper foot for sewing machine

—Gadget Messenger Bag templates on Pattern Insert

FINISHED SIZE

—14" × 12" × 4" (35.5 × 30.5 × 10 cm), excluding strap

NOTES

—All seam allowances are ½" (1.3 cm) unless otherwise noted.

—Edgestitch ⅛" (3 mm) from the edge unless otherwise noted.

—Leave small peripherals, such as flash drives and wireless receivers, plugged into the hub in the patch pocket and plug them all into the computer at once by connecting the hub cable from where it exits the bag at the side. To charge a laptop or other device in the main compartment of the bag, run its power cord through the pass-through cable outlet in the side.

—The bellows pocket was sized to fit a particular USB hub, adjust the dimensions and depth of this pocket to fit the hub you intend to use. You may also want to alter the placement of the bellows pocket's cable outlet, depending on where the cord connects to your hub.

—The bag is sized to fit a laptop with a 13" (33 cm) screen (measured diagonally), with generous space for files, books, etc. For further protection of the computer, use a padded laptop sleeve as well.

—Instead of a typical bag glide with a center bar, two rectangular key rings from the hardware store are used for the adjustable strap.

Since the two rings are separate and not fixed flat like a bag glide, the strap is woven through them several times to produce the tension necessary to hold the strap at the desired length.

—For a stiffer bag bottom, insert a piece of cardboard or ultra-firm interfacing inside the bag before lining the bag, gluing the cardboard, or sewing the interfacing to the bottom side seam allowances.

CUT THE FABRIC

1 It may be helpful to label cut pieces with a removable fabric pen or pieces of tape.

From the duck canvas, cut the following pieces:

—43" × 15" (109 × 38 cm) Main Shell

—Two 13" × 5" (33 × 12.5 cm) Shell Sides

—Two 7½" × 15" (19 × 38 cm) Pocket Panels

—Two 4½" × 6½" (11.5 × 16.5 cm) Bellows Pocket Pieces

—Two 2¾" × 12" (7 × 30.5 cm) Short Straps

—Two 2¾" × 60" (7 × 152.5 cm) Long Straps

—2" × 5" (5 × 12.5 cm) Channel Facing

Cut a piece of interfacing for each canvas piece, subtracting ¾" (2 cm) from each dimension to reduce bulk in the seam allowances. Fuse each interfacing piece to the wrong side of the corresponding canvas piece, following the manufacturer's instructions.

From the ripstop nylon, cut the following pieces:

—15" × 15" (38 × 38 cm) Flap Lining

—29" × 15" (73.5 × 38 cm) Main Lining

—Two 13" × 5" (33 × 12.5 cm) Lining Sides

—From the contrast cotton fabric cut:

—Four 2¾" × 1" (7 × 2.5 cm) Strap End pieces

2 Trace the USB Motif template onto the paper side of the fusible web. Cut the shape out roughly, leaving a ¼" (6 mm) margin on all sides. Fuse the shape to the wrong side of the remaining contrast cotton fabric, following the manufacturer's instructions, then cut the shape out along the lines.

APPLIQUÉ THE USB MOTIF

3 Remove the paper backing and fuse the contrast fabric USB Motif to the right side of one end of the canvas Main Shell piece, referring to the photo above for guidance. The slanted base of the appliqué will lie along one 15" (38 cm) edge of the canvas piece, beginning about 2" (5 cm) from the long left edge. Adjust the placement slightly, if desired, but keep the seam allowances in mind. Using thread matching the motif, sew around the edges with a zigzag stitch 1 mm long and 1.5–2 mm wide. The outer swing of the needle should fall just outside the contrast motif in the canvas background, with the bulk of the stitch on the motif itself. Pivot with the needle in the fabric outside the motif on outside curves and corners, or inside the motif on inside curves and corners.

CONSTRUCT THE POCKETS AND CORD CHANNEL

4 Using a ¼" (6 mm) seam allowance, sew the Bellows Pocket pieces right sides together, leaving an opening in the center of one long side. Trim the corners diagonally to reduce bulk and turn the pocket right side out, folding the seam allowances to the wrong side at the opening. Edgestitch both long sides, closing the gap as you stitch. Press ⅞" (2.2 cm) to the wrong side along both short pocket edges, then press ½" (1.3 cm) back to the right side, accordion style (**figure 1**).

5 Pin the assembled Bellows Pocket right side up on the right side of one of the canvas Pocket Panel pieces, placing the Bellows Pocket 1½" (3.8 cm) from the left and top edges of the Pocket Panel. Edgestitch the sides and bottom of the Bellows Pocket to secure it to the Pocket Panel. Backtack at the beginning and end of the

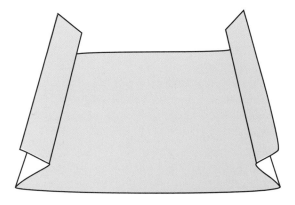

figure 1

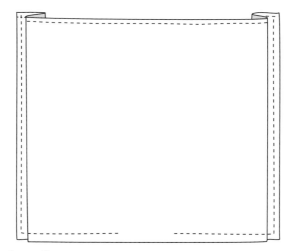

figure 2

edgestitches, and leave a 1" (2.5 cm) opening at the center of the bottom edge for the hub cable to exit. Catch the pleats on the Bellows Pocket (made in previous step) in the stitching along the pocket bottom, but not along the sides (**figure 2**).

6 Sew a 1" (2.5 cm) long buttonhole parallel to the bottom of the Bellows Pocket, centered on the pocket and 1¼" (3.2 cm) from the bottom edge of the Pocket Panel. Carefully open the buttonhole with small sharp scissors or a seam ripper.

7 Cut a 15" (38 cm) length of corded piping and pin it to one long side of the remaining Pocket Panel piece, right sides together, with raw edges matched and the piping seam lying along the Pocket Panel seam line. To reduce bulk in later seams, remove a few stitches holding the piping closed and trim ½" (1.3 cm) of the filling cord away at each end, then reposition the empty end of the piping fabric. Using a zipper foot to sew close to the piping, baste it in place. With the piped panel on top, sew the two Pocket Panels right sides together just inside the basting stitches (closer to the cord), again using the zipper foot. Sew the opposite long edges together with a ¼" (6 mm) seam allowance, then pink or zigzag-stitch the seam allowances to prevent fraying when pushing the USB cable through the channel. Turn the assembled Pocket Panel right side out and press.

8 Pin the Pocket Panel, with the Bellows Pocket on top, to the right side of the Main Shell piece, at the end opposite the appliquéd motif, placing the corded top edge of the pocket panel 1½" (3.8 cm) from the end of the Main Shell. Baste the raw side edges of the pocket panel to the Main Shell piece, ⅜" (1 cm) from the raw edges. Edgestitch the bottom of the pocket panel.

9 Draw a removable guideline parallel to the bottom edge of the Pocket Panel and ¼" (6 mm) above the buttonhole. Topstitch along the guideline to create the cable channel. Measure and draw removable guidelines parallel to the side of the Bellows Pocket 1½" (3.8 cm) and 3¼" (8.5 cm) from the right-hand edge of the Bellows Pocket, dividing the Pocket Panel into smaller pockets, or place the dividing lines as desired to make pockets to suit your gear. Topstitch along each line from the corded edge of the Pocket Panel to the upper edge of the channel.

10 Cut two 2" (5 cm) lengths of hook-and-loop tape. Position the loop side of one piece 1½" (3.8 cm) from the left edge of the Main Shell, abutting the Pocket Panel, and edgestitch to secure. Repeat to position the second loop piece 1½" (3.8 cm) from the right edge of the Main Shell.

11 Clip into the Main Shell's seam allowance on the left-hand edge just inside the topstitching that defines the cable channel, making each cut a little less than the ½" (1.3 cm) seam allowance (⁷⁄₁₆" [1.1 cm]). Fold the resulting tab to the wrong side and finger-press (**figure 3**).

CONSTRUCT THE STRAPS AND SIDES

12 Using a ¼" (6 mm) seam allowance, sew a contrast Strap End piece to one end of each canvas Short and Long Strap piece with right sides together. Press the seam allowances toward the contrast fabric.

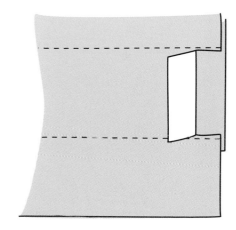

figure 3

13 Sew each pair of corresponding Strap pieces right sides together along both long sides with ½" (1.3 cm) seam allowances, pivoting to sew across the contrast end just outside the previous seam allowances (¼" [6 mm] from the seam). Trim the corners diagonally and turn the straps right side out. Fold ½" (1.3 cm) to the wrong side at the open end of each assembled strap and press. Edgestitch both long edges of the long strap only.

14 Insert the open end of the short strap through a rectangular metal ring, fold the end of the strap to the wrong side around one edge of the ring, and topstitch along the Strap's folded end through all thicknesses. Pin the Strap, centered, right side up on the right side of one of the canvas Shell Sides, placing the contrast end 2" (5 cm) from the bottom short end of the Shell Side; the metal ring will extend beyond the upper end of the Side piece. Edgestitch the strap to the Shell Side along one long side of the Strap, stopping ¾" (2 cm) from the top edge of the Side piece. Pivot with the needle down and stitch across the Strap, then pivot again to edgestitch the second long edge. Pivot again at the contrast fabric to stitch in the ditch across the Strap, then pivot a final time to return to the starting point. Topstitch a 1" (2.5 cm) reinforcing square in the center of the Strap 1¼" (3.2 cm) from the top edge of the Shell Side and ¼" (6 mm) from the Strap edgestitching.

15 On the remaining canvas Shell Side piece, sew a 1⅛" (3 cm) long buttonhole 2" (5 cm) from the right-hand long edge, starting 5½" (14 cm) from the bottom of the piece. Pin the Channel Facing over the buttonhole, wrong sides up, with the short ends of the Facing aligned with the long sides of the Shell Side piece. Check that at least ¼" (6 mm) of the Facing extends above and below the buttonhole, then topstitch the Facing to the Side piece, ¼" (6 mm) from each long side of the Facing. Sew an identical buttonhole through both Side and Facing, 2" (5 cm) from the left edge of the Side piece (this pass-through outlet will be accessible to the main interior of the bag). Cut a 1¼" (3.2 cm) strip of hook-and-loop tape. Place the loop

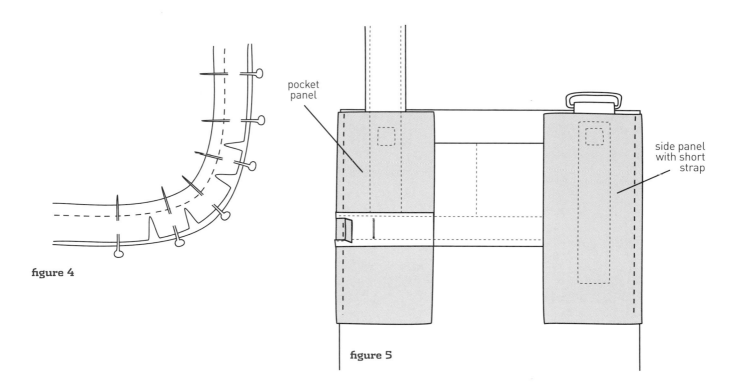

pocket
panel

side panel
with short
strap

figure 4

figure 5

side on the Shell Side, centered below the buttonholes and aligned with the lowest line of topstitching on the Side piece; edgestitch in place.

16 Edgestitch the hook portion of the 1¼" (3.2 cm) hook-and-loop tape to the back of the long Strap, 1¼" (3.2 cm) from the contrast end. Fasten the tape to position the Strap on the Side piece, with the contrast end 2" (5 cm) from the bottom end of the Side piece. Edgestitch the Strap to the Side, beginning at the upper line of topstitching for the side channel and sewing directly on top of the previous edgestitching. Stop sewing and backtack 1" (2.5 cm) below the upper edge of the Side. Begin edgestitching the other side of the Strap 1" (2.5 cm) below the upper edge, ending at the upper line of topstitching; the end will be left loose as a flap to cover the cable outlets and closed by the hook-and-loop tape. Sew a reinforcing square as in Step 17.

ASSEMBLE THE SHELL

17 Use the Corner template to trim the Main Shell corners at the end with the appliqué. Pin corded piping to the Main Shell piece, right sides together, along the long sides and the short end with the appliqué, with the raw edges together and the piping seam along the shell seam line. At the corners, clip into the

seam allowance of the cording to ease into a smooth curve (**figure 4**). Remove the filling cord from the ends and baste the cording as described in Step 10, shortening the stitch length when sewing around the corners. Make sure the folded-back tab at the cable channel is not caught in the stitching.

18 Pin the Shell Side pieces to the Main Shell, right sides together, with the upper edges of the Sides aligned with the pocket end of the Main Shell (**figure 5**). Clip and fold the channel facing seam allowance as described in Step 14 where the side channel meets the pocket panel channel. Using a zipper foot, sew the side pieces to the Main Shell close to the corded piping, stopping and backtacking ½" (1.3 cm) from the bottom edge of the side pieces. Make sure the channel tab is not caught in the seam.

19 Clip the Main Shell seam allowance to the end of the stitching on each side, being careful not to clip the stitches or cut beyond the seam line. Fold the Main Shell around the corner and align it with the bottom edge of the side piece, right sides together, to form the bottom of the bag. Sew as described in the previous step, backtacking to start and stop ½" (1.3 cm) from the edges.

20 Repeat the previous step to form the shell back by joining the remaining long edges of the side pieces to the Main Shell, stopping ½" (1.3 cm) from the upper edge of the side pieces. The flap will extend past the shell front and sides. Press the seams to one side.

21 Trim the side seam allowances at the cable channel to ¼" (6 mm) and whipstitch them together. Whipstitch the folded-back tabs together along the folds.

ASSEMBLE THE LINING

22 Following the process for sewing the shell pieces together, sew the Lining Sides to the Main lining. Sew all the way to the raw edges at the top of the lining.

23 Topstitch the hook portions of the 2" (5 cm) hook-and-loop tape remaining from the shell front to the flap lining, placing each piece 1" (2.5 cm) from the bottom of the lining and 1½" (3.8 cm) in from each side edge.

24 Pin the Flap lining to the shell flap, right sides together, positioning the hook-and-loop tape side along the curved edge of the flap. Using a zipper foot, sew the shell and Flap Lining together close to the cord, starting and stopping 1" (2.5 cm) from the shell side pieces and shortening the stitch length to sew around the corners. Round the lining corners to match the shell ; clip and grade the curved seam allowances.

25 Insert the shell into the lining, right sides together, keeping the flap out of the way and making sure the Straps are between the shell and the lining. Sew the lining to the shell around the raw side and front edges, leaving the flap/back side open. Be careful not to catch the Straps in the stitching. Turn the bag right side out through the opening at the flap. Turn the flap right side out, press, and tuck the lining seam allowance (where the flap meets the bag) behind the main lining. Fold ½" (1.3 cm) to the wrong side along the open edge of the bag lining, pin, and topstitch through all layers to close the opening.

26 Topstitch around the upper edges of the bag, continuing the line of stitching that closed the flap opening. For a clean finish, backtack on either side of the piping that would intersect the stitching instead of sewing over it. Topstitch around the flap inside the piped edge, closing any gaps in the seam just above the main portion of the bag (from Step 27).

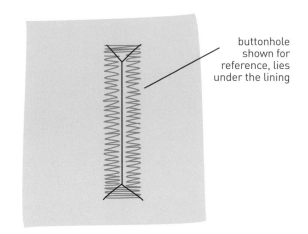

buttonhole shown for reference, lies under the lining

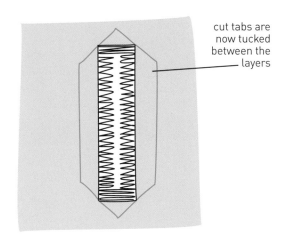

cut tabs are now tucked between the layers

figure 6

27 Pin the lining to the shell around the pass-through buttonhole on the side of the bag (the one that extends through both layers of the channel). Carefully slit the lining through the buttonhole, beginning and ending ¼" (6 mm) from the ends of the buttonhole. From the inside, clip the lining diagonally from the ends of the slit to the buttonhole corners (**figure 6**) to make small triangular tabs at each end of the slit, extending them just a few threads past the buttonhole. Tuck the tabs between the lining and the shell and whipstitch the folds to the Channel Facing.

FINISH THE STRAPS

28 Insert the loose end of the long Strap through the two remaining square rings, then insert it through the ring attached to the short strap. Bring the Strap end back up behind the Strap and through the uppermost ring from top to bottom. Weave the Strap end from bottom to top through the middle ring. Fold ½" (1.3 cm) of the Strap end to the wrong side. Fold the Strap to the wrong side again ½" (1.3 cm) below the previous fold, trapping the middle ring between the folds. Edgestitch the first fold to the main part of the Strap, then edgestitch close to the second fold to secure the middle ring (**figure 7**). Use a large needle (size 100/16) and stitch slowly, turning the hand wheel manually if necessary, to pierce the many layers of canvas.

29 Place the USB hub in the bellows pocket, orienting the ports to be accessible from the pocket opening. Bring the cable through the opening at the bottom of the pocket, then insert the end into the cable channel through the buttonhole. Carefully work the cable end through the channel on the pocket panel, past the side seam and into the side channel, and out through the buttonhole on the side. When not in use, the cable end will be covered by the flap at the end of the long strap.

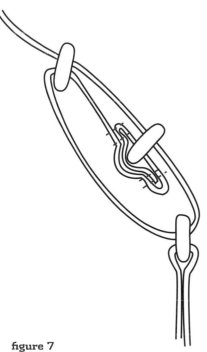

figure 7

The unique pleated handles make a fun design element on this wool-felt handbag, with insets that add a pop of color. An adjustable strap pulls in the sides of the bag to give it its elegant shape, and roomy pockets on the sides make it easy to carry all your essentials. *by* **AYUMI TAKAHASHI**

pleats please BAG

FABRIC

—1 yd (91.5 cm) of 36" (91.5 cm) wide wool blend felt for main bag (Main)

—¼ yd (23 cm) of 45" (114.5 cm) wide cotton print for handle insets (A; *shown:* teal Paris print)

—½ yd (45.5 cm) of 45" (114.5 cm) wide cotton print for main handles (B; *shown:* black writing print)

—7/8 yd (80 cm) of 45" (114.5 cm) wide cotton print for lining (C; *shown:* pastel green Paris print)

—¼ yd (23 cm) of 45" (114.5 cm) wide cotton print for interior strap (D; *shown:* white/gray stripe)

OTHER SUPPLIES

—Cotton sewing thread to match main felt

—Cotton sewing thread to match main handles

—Handsewing needle

—1" (2.5 cm) long piece of Velcro™

—Two 1" (2.5 cm) D rings

—Rotary cutter, rigid acrylic ruler, and self-healing mat

FINISHED SIZE

—About 12" long × 15" wide × 6½" deep (30.5 × 38 × 16.5 cm) without handles. With handles, the bag is about 20" (51 cm) long.

NOTES

—All seam allowances are ¼" (6 mm) unless otherwise noted.

CUT THE FABRIC

1 Cut the following pieces as directed (you may want to label each piece on the wrong side with a removable fabric pen or tape).

From Main fabric, cut:

—Two 15½" × 12½" (39.5 × 31.5 cm) rectangles for Front/Back Panels

—Two 12½" × 7" (31.5 × 18 cm) rectangles for Side Panels

—One 15½" × 7" (39.5 × 18 cm) rectangle for Bottom Panel

—Two 6½" × 11½" (16.5 × 29 cm) rectangles for Pockets

From fabric A, cut:

—Two 3" × 42" (7.5 × 106.5 cm) strips for Handle Insets

From fabric B, cut:

—Two 8" × 42" (20.5 × 106.5 cm) strips for Main Handles

From fabric C, cut:

—Two 15½" × 12½" (39.5 × 31.5 cm) rectangles for Front and Back Lining Panels

—Two 12½" × 7" (31.5 × 18 cm) rectangles for Side Lining Panels

—One 15½" × 7" (39.5 × 18 cm) rectangle for Bottom Lining Panel

From fabric D, cut:

—Two 4" × 10½" (10 × 26.5 cm) strips for Interior Strap

MAKE THE HANDLES

2 Fold the fabric B Main Handles in half widthwise, with wrong sides together. At the raw short edge, mark 2½" (6.5 cm) in from each long edge so that the distance between the two marks is 3" (7.5 cm). Mark 10" (25.5 cm) from the raw short edge on both long edges. Use a ruler to connect each short-edge mark with the corresponding long-edge mark (**figure 1**). Cut along these lines through both layers of fabric so each end of the strip is tapered. Repeat this entire step to taper the ends of the remaining Main Handle.

3 Pin one prepared Main Handle (from Step 2) and one fabric A Handle Inset piece along both long edges with right sides together, easing the Main Handle edges to match those of the inset. Sew both long edges. Turn right side out and press with the fabric A

inset centered. Fold the main handle fabric toward the inset fabric at the seams and press; the Main Handle will meet in the middle with the inset exposed at each end of the handle. Repeat the entire step for the remaining Main Handle and Handle Inset piece to make a second handle.

ASSEMBLE THE SHELL

4 Align the short ends of one handle with a long edge of a Main fabric Front/Back Panel with the handle ends 2½" (6.5 cm) from the short outer edges, inset sides up, and pin in place. Edgestitch the handle's long edges from the bottom of the insets for 10" (25.5 cm), using cotton sewing thread to match

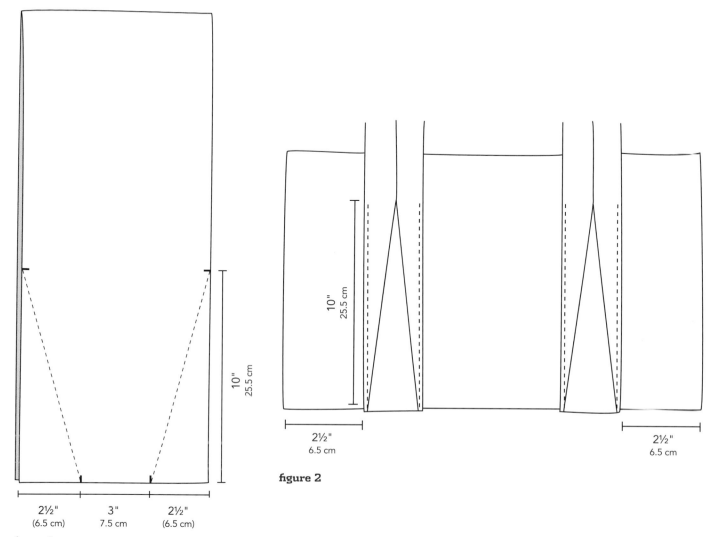

10"
25.5 cm

2½"
(6.5 cm)   3"   2½"
           7.5 cm   (6.5 cm)

figure 1

10"
25.5 cm

2½"
6.5 cm

2½"
6.5 cm

figure 2

the handles (**figure 2**). Repeat this entire step to join the remaining handle to the remaining Main fabric Front/Back Panel.

5 Pin one Side Panel to a Front/Back Panel with right sides together and the Side Panel's long edge aligned with the Front/Back Panel's short edge. Sew along the aligned edge. In the same manner, sew the remaining Side Panel to the opposite edge of the same Front/Back Panel, then sew the free short edges of the remaining Front/Back Panel to the free raw long edges of the Side Panels. You have now created the bag shell (there is no bottom to the bag yet).

6 Position one Pocket piece right side up on one side panel of the assembled bag shell, aligning the bottom

✚ Try using outdoor fabrics for your next bag; these fabrics are often treated with ultraviolet filters and protective coatings to repel moisture and dirt. They're stiff enough to give your bags a great shape. —**APRIL MOFFATT**

edges; the short edges of the Pocket should extend past the side seams to meet the handles on the front and back panels. Edgestitch both short Pocket edges and the bottom edge using matching thread. Repeat this entire step to attach the remaining Pocket to the opposite side of the bag (refer to the photo on opposite page).

7 With right sides together, pin the Main fabric Bottom Panel to the assemble bag shell (created in Steps 5 and 6), aligning the shell's side seams with the corners of the Bottom Panel. Sew together one edge at a time, starting and stopping ¼" (6 mm) in from the ends. Backtack at both ends of each seam. Because the Pockets wrap around the side seams, you may need to ease the corners of the shell so the seams are smooth.

8 Fold a fabric D Interior Strap in half lengthwise with wrong sides together. Open the strip and fold the two long edges toward the folded line in the middle and press. Refold the strip along the center and press. Edgestitch both long edges. Cut a 3" (7.5 cm) length from the sewn strip. Then fold the 3" (7.5 cm) strip in half widthwise and lace through one D ring. Aligning the raw edges, pin this piece to the center top edge of one of the shell bag's Side Panels and sew very close to the edge to attach it. Repeat this entire step to attach a D ring strap to the opposite Side Panel. Set aside the longer strap pieces.

ASSEMBLE THE LINING

9 Repeat Steps 5–7 to create the lining bag, leaving a 5" (12.5 cm) opening in one of the bottom seams. With the shell wrong side out, insert the lining inside with right sides together, sandwiching the D ring straps inside. Sew the top edge together and turn the bag right side out through the opening in the bottom, being careful not to catch the handles. Handsew the opening closed with a slip stitch. Topstitch ⅛" (3 mm) from the upper edge of the bag, again being careful not to catch the handles.

10 On the parts of the handles that extend beyond the top edge of the bag, bring the outer edges of the handles together to meet in the middle; keeping the center of the strap out of the way, edgestitch the two outer edges closed, backtacking at both ends (**figure 3**).

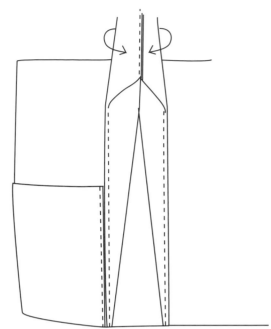

figure 3

11 Lace one of the long strap pieces set aside in Step 8 through each of the D rings attached at the top of the bag. Turn under each short end by ¼" (6 mm), then sew the two ends together on each strap. Position half of the Velcro™ on the top of one long strap near the end opposite the D ring, then topstitch in place. Sew the remaining half of the Velcro™ to the bottom of the remaining long strap so the straps will attach with an overlap.

BAG CONSTRUCTION
tips + tricks

Handbag, purse, clutch, tote, or carryall, you just never have enough of these useful accessories! Use the following tips the next time you feel inspired to stitch up a bag.

CONSIDER THE STRESS POINTS
Think about how your bag will be used. Will you be toting heavy loads? Will you be storing the bag by hanging it from a hook? Make sure that your stitching is strong enough to withstand the wear and tear of everyday use. Here are some techniques to strengthen your tote:

■ Double stitch (stitch the first seam, then stitch again within the seam allowance, $\frac{1}{16}$–$\frac{1}{8}$" [2–3 mm] from the first seam line) and/or topstitch seams (catching the seam allowances in the stitching) to add strength. Try using a contrasting thread to make topstitching an eye-catching design element.

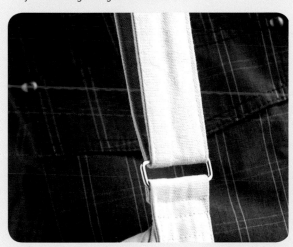

■ To attach exposed straps or handles, topstitch a square on the strap/handle, then topstitch an × shape through the middle of the square.
■ Bartack or use a short zigzag stitch at the top corners of patch pockets to reinforce the attachment.

ORGANIZE YOUR ESSENTIALS
Most of us have lots of little things we carry around that can easily become lost in the depths of a handbag. If you plan to use your bag to carry things such as a cell phone, pens, makeup, and other loose items, consider adding pockets, so you can easily find what you need. Here are some tips to make sure your pockets serve their purpose well:

■ Topstitch lines from the top to the bottom of a pocket to quickly create divided slots for multiple items that are about the same length.
■ Create a separate pocket just for your cell phone. Measure the length, width, and depth (thickness) of your cell phone and record the measurements. To ensure that your phone will fit into the pocket, you'll want to add about twice the depth measurement to the width. This is the spacing you'll need between the stitch lines attaching the pocket to the bag. Remember that you'll also need to fit the length of the phone between the bottom stitching on the pocket and the top of the pocket.
■ In the side seam near the top edge of the bag, sew a length of sturdy cord or trim to create a small loop. Use a keychain clip to attach your house or car key to the loop for quick access.

LINE THE BAG FOR FUN AND USE
A lining is a fun place to feature a brightly-colored contrasting fabric or a fantastic print. Even if the outside of your bag is all business, the inside is for your eyes only, so pick a lining fabric that you love. Here are some other things to consider when choosing a lining fabric:

■ Avoid delicate or loosely woven fabrics prone to snagging. The lining of your bag will be exposed to all of the items you carry, so the fabric needs to be able to withstand the normal jostling of items.

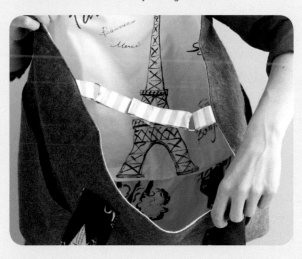

■ If your bag will be used for carrying food and drink or other liquids such as sunscreen or makeup, consider using a water-resistant or waterproof lining fabric (such as rip-stop nylon or laminated cotton) for easy cleanup in case of a spill.

GUIDE TO *interfacing*

Interfacing is a support fabric used in areas requiring stability and more body than the fabric itself.

THE BASICS
There are three types of interfacing—woven, knitted, and nonwoven—available in several weights and in white, black, gray, and/or beige.

- Woven interfacings have lengthwise and crosswise grains that should be matched to the garment fabric. They offer stability in both directions, but woven interfacings are often cut on the bias when used with knits or in areas requiring some drape. A specialty woven interfacing called hair canvas is designed for tailoring projects.

- Nonwoven interfacings are made by bonding fibers together, creating a flat appearance. They can be cut without regard to grain and tend to be less drapable than other types.

Fusible interfacing attached to the wrong side of the fabric (Perfect Fuse medium-weight interfacing).

- Knit interfacings are soft and supple, adding just a hint of structure to fashion fabric. They're often used to back an entire garment section to help reduce wrinkling and to add more body to a soft fabric. A specialty type of knit interfacing is called weft insertion, meaning that an extra set of threads is added to increase body.

GETTING IT ON
- Interfacings can be attached two ways: sewing or fusing. Sew-in interfacing is caught to the project fabric only in or near the seam lines, whereas fusible is attached throughout the piece by activating the adhesive dots with heat and steam from an iron.

- Fusible interfacings are the easiest to use, but they're not appropriate for some fabrics, especially those that are lightweight and sheer because the adhesive dot patterning can show through. Napped fabrics such as velvet and corduroy don't work well with fusibles because the heat and pressure needed for fusing damages the pile.

CHOOSING THE RIGHT INTERFACING
- Interfacing should be similar in weight to the fashion fabric and complement it when applied. Fusibles tend to add a bit more body than comparable weight sew-ins simply because of the adhesive.

- Choose a color similar to the fabric tone—light color interfacing with light color fabric and so on. Place a scrap of interfacing under your fabric and check for any visible color change. In some instances, beige may be a better choice than white. It's good to have several types and colors of interfacing in your stash for testing.

- Before committing to an interfacing, test it with the fabric. Cut a 6" to 12" (15 to 30.5 cm) square and following the manufacturer's instructions attach it to a same-size scrap of your project fabric. Drape the duo over your hand and see whether it adds the support and stability for the look you want. If not, try another type. The interfacing should not overpower the fabric itself, but simply complement it.

PRESHRINKING

■ Just as you would pretreat your fashion fabric, preshrink your interfacing as well. If you don't, you could end up with bubbles and puckers after the first laundering, because many interfacings do shrink.

■ Soak it for about ten minutes in a basin of warm water and lay it flat on a towel to dry. You can also steam-shrink a sew-in by holding the iron over it for several minutes. Nonwovens don't need pretreating.

CUTTING UP

■ When you purchase interfacing, be sure to note the width, because most interfacings are narrower than fashion fabrics.

■ Pattern guide sheets tell you which pieces to cut from interfacing, and in some instances, there are dedicated pattern pieces for interfacing only. Follow the same grain on woven or knit interfacings as the corresponding garment section.

■ Transfer pattern markings to the cut pieces, because once the interfacing is applied, you'll cover any markings put on the garment area wrong side.

■ If desired, trim ¼" to ⅜" (6 mm to 1 cm) off the outer edges of the interfacing pieces and trim corners diagonally—both tactics help reduce bulk.

READY, SET, ATTACH

■ Interfacing is always applied to the fabric wrong side before construction begins.

■ For fusible interfacings, follow the manufacturer's instructions for applying—most recommend a press cloth and steam; some require a damp press cloth. Fuse completely from both sides, overlapping the iron positioning to avoid any bubbling, and let the pieces cool in place before moving them from the ironing board.

■ For sew-ins, hand or machine baste the interfacing to its fabric counterpart just inside the seam line or foldline. For a quicker application, use a washable glue stick to hold it in place until subsequent construction catches it in the stitching line.

TYPES OF KNIT INTERFACING

1. French Fuse (Staple Sewing Aids) **2.** Hair Canvas (Tailor's Pride from HTCW Products) **3.** Nonwoven interfacing (Pel-aire from Pellon) **4.** Woven interfacing (Armo Press from HTCW Products) **5.** Weft insertion (Ultraweft from Pellon)

sewing basics

sewing kit

The following items are essential for your sewing kit. Make sure you have these tools at hand before starting any of the projects:

ACRYLIC RULER This is a clear flat ruler, with a measuring grid at least 2" (5 cm) wide × 18" (45.5 cm) long. A rigid acrylic (quilter's) ruler should be used when working with a rotary cutter.

CLOTH MEASURING TAPE Make sure it's at least 60" (152.5 cm) long.

CRAFT SCISSORS Use these for cutting out paper patterns.

DRESSMAKER'S SHEARS These sharp long-bladed scissors are used to cut fabric.

EMBROIDERY SCISSORS These small scissors are used to trim off threads, clip corners, and do other intricate cutting work.

FABRIC MARKING PENS/PENCILS + TAILOR'S CHALK Available in several colors for use on light and dark fabrics; use them for tracing patterns and pattern markings onto your fabric. Tailor's chalk is available in triangular pieces, rollers, and pencils. Some forms (such as powdered) can simply be brushed away; refer to manufacturer's instructions for the recommended removal method for your chosen marking tool.

HANDSEWING + EMBROIDERY NEEDLES Keep an assortment of sewing and embroidery needles in different sizes, from fine to sturdy.

IRON, IRONING BOARD + PRESS CLOTHS An iron is an essential tool when sewing. Use cotton muslin or silk organza as a press cloth to protect delicate fabric surfaces from direct heat.

PATTERN PAPER Have some pattern paper or other large paper (such as newsprint, butcher paper, or pattern tracing cloth) on hand for tracing the patterns you intend to use from the pattern insert. Regular office paper may be used for templates that will fit.

SEAM GAUGE This small ruler with a movable slider is used for marking hems, checking seam allowances, placing buttons, and more.

SEAM RIPPER Handy for quickly ripping out stitches.

SPIKED TRACING WHEEL + COLORED TRACING PAPER Use these tools for tracing patterns and markings onto your fabric.

STRAIGHT PINS + PINCUSHION Always keep lots of pins nearby.

WEIGHTS Pattern weights or small rocks are great for keeping fabric in place while drawing, pinning, and cutting.

optional . . .
but good to have.

FRENCH CURVE A template of metal, plastic, or wood that includes many curved edges for constructing smooth curves.

NEEDLE THREADER An inexpensive aid to make threading the eye of the needle super fast.

PINKING SHEARS These scissors with notched teeth leave a zigzag edge on the cut cloth to prevent fraying.

POINT TURNER A bluntly pointed tool that helps push out the corners of a project and/or smooth seams. A knitting needle or chopstick can also be used.

ROTARY CUTTER + SELF-HEALING MAT Useful for cutting out fabric quickly. Always use the mat to protect the blade and your work surface (a rigid acrylic ruler should be used with these to make straight cuts).

TAILOR'S HAM A firm cushion used when pressing curved areas to preserve the shape and prevent creases.

THIMBLE Your fingers and thumbs will thank you.

ZIPPER FOOT This accessory foot for your machine has a narrow profile that can be positioned to sew close to the zipper teeth. Zipper feet are adjustable, so the foot can be moved to either side of the needle.

PATTERN INSERT GUIDE A quick reference to the full-size patterns and the symbols and markings on the patterns.

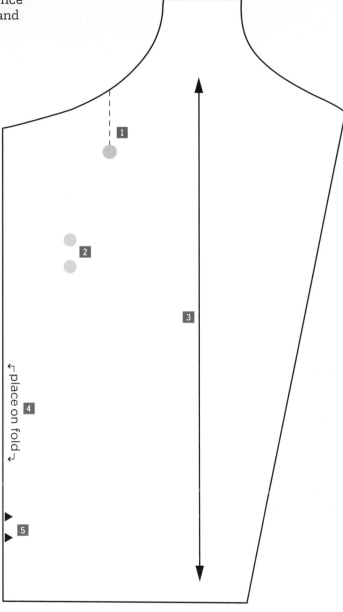

1 PLEATS Match the notches by folding the fabric, following the direction of the arrows, to form pleats.

2 PATTERN DOTS Filled circles indicate that a mark needs to be made (often on the right side of the fabric), for placement of elements such as a pocket or a dart point. Mark by punching through the pattern paper only, then mark on the fabric through the hole.

3 GRAINLINE The double-ended arrow should be parallel to the lengthwise grain or fold unless marked as crosswise. A bias grainline will be diagonal and will be marked "bias".

4 PLACE ON FOLD BRACKET This is a grainline marking with arrows pointing to the edge of the pattern. Place the pattern edge on the fold of the fabric so that your finished piece will be twice the size of the pattern piece, without having to add a seam. Do not cut the fold.

5 NOTCHES Notches are triangle-shaped symbols used for accurately matching seams. Pieces to be joined will have corresponding notches.

layout, marking + cutting guidelines

- The pattern insert often features overlapping patterns, so you may not want to cut patterns or templates directly from the insert. Instead, use pattern paper (or other paper such as newsprint) or pattern tracing cloth to trace the pattern pieces you need from the insert and then cut out your traced pieces. Regular office paper may be used for small templates that will fit. If necessary, use a light box or bright window for tracing.
- If you are cutting pattern pieces on the fold or cutting two of the same pattern piece, fold the fabric in half, selvedge to selvedge (or fold as shown in the cutting layouts), with right sides together.
- All pattern markings should be on the wrong side of the fabric unless otherwise noted.
- Lay the pattern pieces on the fabric as close together as possible. Double-check that all pattern pieces cut "on the fold" are placed on the fold.
- Make sure all pattern pieces are placed on the fabric with the grainline running parallel to the lengthwise grain, unless a bias grainline is present or as otherwise noted.
- Use weights to hold the pattern pieces down and use pins to secure the corners as needed.
- Cut pieces slowly and carefully.

GLOSSARY OF SEWING TERMS + TECHNIQUES
A quick reference to the technical sewing terms used throughout the project instructions.

BACKTACK STITCHING done in reverse for a short distance at the beginning and ending of a seam line to secure the stitches. Most machines have a button or knob for this function (also called backstitch).

BARTACK A line of reinforcement stitching often placed at areas of stress on a garment. Bartacks are created with short zigzag stitches (by machine) or whipstitches (by hand).

BASTING Uses long, loose stitches to hold something in place temporarily. To baste by machine, use the longest straight stitch length available on your machine. To baste by hand, use stitches at least ¼" (6 mm) long. Use a contrasting thread to make the stitches easier to spot for removal.

BIAS The direction across a fabric that is located at a 45-degree angle from the lengthwise or crosswise grain. The bias has high stretch and a very fluid drape.

BIAS TAPE Made from fabric strips cut on a 45-degree angle to the grainline, the bias cut creates an edging fabric that will stretch to enclose smooth or curved edges. You can buy bias tape ready-made or make your own.

BUTTONHOLES To determine the length of your buttonhole, first measure the button across the width and then add ⅛" (3 mm). Some thicker buttons may require adding ¼" (6 mm) to the width measurement. Mark this measurement with a fabric pencil where you want the buttonhole placed; always sew a sample buttonhole on scrap fabric to test the measurement.

CLIPPING CURVES Involves cutting tiny slits or triangles into the seam allowance of curved edges, so the seam will lie flat when turned right side out. Cut slits along concave curves and triangles (with points toward the seam line) along a convex curve. Be careful not to clip into the stitches.

CLIP THE CORNERS Clipping the corners of a project reduces bulk and allows for crisper corners in the finished project. To clip a corner, cut off a triangle-shaped piece of fabric across the seam allowances at the corner. Cut close to the seam line but be careful not to cut through the stitches.

EASE/EASE IN When a pattern directs to "ease" or "ease in," you are generally sewing a longer piece of fabric to a shorter piece or a curved piece to a straight piece. This creates shape in a garment or object without pleats or gathers. To ease, match the ends or notches of the uneven section and pin together (or pin as instructed by the pattern). Continue to pin the remaining fabric together, distributing the extra fullness evenly, but making sure that the seam lines match up as smoothly as possible (you will be smoothing the excess fullness away from the edge); don't be afraid to use a lot of pins. Stitch slowly, smoothing as necessary to ease the pieces together as evenly as possible, being careful not to catch tucks in the seam.

EDGESTITCH A row of topstitching placed very close (1⁄16–⅛" [2–3 mm]) to an edge or an existing seam line.

FABRIC GRAIN The grain is created in a woven fabric by the threads that travel lengthwise and crosswise. The lengthwise grain runs parallel to the selvedges; the crosswise grain should always be perpendicular to the lengthwise threads. If the grains aren't completely straight and perpendicular, grasp the fabric at diagonally opposite corners and pull gently to restore the grain. In knit fabrics, the lengthwise grain runs along the wales (ribs), parallel to the selvedges, with the crosswise grain running along the courses (perpendicular to the wales).

FINGER-PRESS Pressing a fold or crease with your fingers as opposed to using an iron.

GRAINLINE A pattern marking showing the direction of the grain. Make sure the grainline marked on the pattern runs parallel to the lengthwise grain of your fabric, unless the grainline is specifically marked as crosswise or bias.

LINING The inner fabric of a garment or bag, used to create a finished interior that covers the raw edges of the seams.

INTERFACING/INTERLINING Material used to stabilize or reinforce fabrics. Fusible interfacing has an adhesive coating on one side that adheres to fabric when ironed. Interlining is an additional fabric layer between the shell and lining, used to change the garment drape or add structure or warmth.

MITER JOINING A seam or fold at an angle that bisects the project corner. Most common is a 45-degree angle, like a picture frame, but shapes other than squares or rectangles will have miters with different angles.

OVERCAST STITCH A machine stitch that wraps around the fabric raw edge to finish edges and prevent raveling. Some sewing machines have several overcast stitch options; consult your sewing machine manual for information on stitch settings and the appropriate presser foot for the chosen stitch (often the standard presser foot can be used). A zigzag stitch can be used as an alternative to finish raw edges if your machine doesn't have an overcast stitch function.

PINK To trim with pinking shears, which cut the edge into a zigzag pattern to reduce fraying.

PRESHRINK Many fabrics shrink when washed; you need to wash, dry, and press all your fabric before you start to sew, following the suggested cleaning method marked on the fabric bolt (keep in mind that the appropriate cleaning method may not be machine washing). Don't skip this step!

RIGHT SIDE The front side, or the side that should be on the outside of a finished garment. On a print fabric, the print will be stronger on the right side of the fabric.

RIGHT SIDES TOGETHER The right sides of two fabric layers should be facing each other.

SATIN STITCH (MACHINE) This is a smooth, completely filled column of zigzag stitches achieved by setting the stitch length to 0.2–0.4 mm. The length setting should be short enough for complete coverage but long enough to prevent bunching and thread buildup.

SEAM ALLOWANCE The amount of fabric between the raw edge and the seam.

SELVEDGE This is the tightly woven border on the lengthwise edges of woven fabric and the finished lengthwise edges of knit fabric.

SHELL The outer fabric of a garment or bag (as opposed to the lining, which will be on the inside).

STITCH IN THE DITCH Press a previously sewn seam open or to one side. Lay the seamed fabric right side up under the presser foot and sew along the seam line "ditch." The stitches will fall between the two fabric pieces and disappear into the seam.

SQUARING UP After you have pieced together a fabric block or section, check to make sure the edges are straight and the measurements are correct. Use a rotary cutter and an acrylic ruler to trim the block if necessary. Because you might trim off the backtacking on seams when you square up, machine-stitch across any trimmed seams to secure.

TOPSTITCH Used to hold pieces firmly in place and/or to add a decorative effect, a topstitch is simply a stitch that can be seen on the outside of the garment or piece. To topstitch, make a line of stitching on the outside (right side) of the piece, usually a set distance from an existing seam.

UNDERLINING Fabric used as a backing for the shell of a garment to add structure and/or aid in shaping. It is also sometimes used to make a transparent fabric opaque. Underlinings are cut to the size and shape of each garment piece and the two are basted together and treated as one during construction.

UNDERSTITCHING A line of stitches placed on a facing (or lining), very near the facing/garment seam. Understitching is used to hold the seam allowances and facing together and to prevent the facing from rolling toward the outside of the garment.

WRONG SIDE The wrong side of the fabric is the underside, or the side that should be on the inside of a finished garment. On a print fabric, the print will be lighter or less obvious on the wrong side of the fabric.

GLOSSARY OF STITCHES

A quick reference to the hand and machine stitches used throughout the project instructions.

BACKSTITCH Working from right to left, bring the needle up at **1** and insert behind the starting point at **2**. Bring the needle up at **3**, repeat by inserting at **1** and bringing the needle up at a point that is a stitch length beyond **3**.

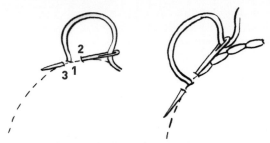

BASTING STITCH (MACHINE)

Using the longest straight stitch length on your machine, baste to temporarily hold fabric layers and seams in position for final stitching. It can also be done by hand. When basting, use a contrasting thread to make it easier to spot when you're taking it out.

BLANKET STITCH

Working from left to right, bring the needle up at **1** and insert at **2**. Bring the needle back up at **3** and over the working thread. Repeat by making the next stitch in the same manner, keeping the spacing even.

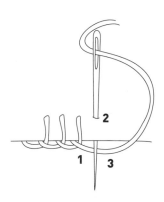

OVERHAND KNOT

Make a loop with the thread. Pass the cord that lies behind the loop over the front cord, then through the loop and pull snug.

STANDARD HAND-APPLIQUÉ STITCH

Cut a length of thread 12" to 18" (30.5 to 45.5 cm) long. Thread the newly cut end through the eye of the needle, pull this end through, and knot it. Use this technique to thread the needle and knot the thread to help keep the thread's "twist" intact and to reduce knotting. Beginning at the straightest edge of the appliqué and working from right to left, bring the needle up from the underside, through the background fabric and the very edge of the appliqué at **1**, catching only a few threads of the appliqué fabric. Pull the thread taut, then insert the needle into the background fabric at **2**, as close as possible to **1**. Bring the needle up through the background fabric at **3**, ⅛" (3 mm) beyond **2**. Continue in this manner, keeping the thread taut (do not pull it so tight that the fabric puckers) to keep the stitching as invisible as possible.

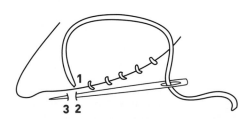

STRAIGHT STITCH + RUNNING STITCH

Working from right to left, make a straight stitch by bringing the needle up and insert at **1**, ⅛" to ¼" (3 to 6 mm) from the starting point. To make a line of running stitches (a row of straight stitches worked one after the other), bring the needle up at **2** and repeat.

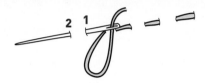

WHIPSTITCH

Bring the needle up at **1**, insert at **2**, and bring up at **3**. These quick stitches do not have to be very tight or close together.

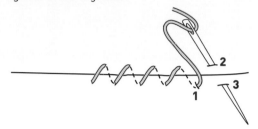

SLIP STITCH

Working from right to left, join two pieces of fabric by taking a ¹⁄₁₆–¼" (2–6 mm) long stitch into the folded edge of one piece of fabric and bringing the needle out. Insert the needle into the folded edge of the other piece of fabric, directly across from the point where the thread emerged from the previous stitch. Repeat by inserting the needle into the first piece of fabric. The thread will be almost entirely hidden inside the folds of the fabrics.

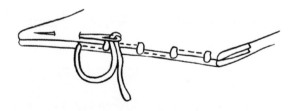

GLOSSARY OF STITCHES
A quick reference to the hand and machine
stitches used throughout the project instructions.

BINDING TECHNIQUES

A quick reference to creating your own
binding.

CUTTING STRAIGHT STRIPS

Cut strips on the crosswise grain, from selvedge to
selvedge, cutting to the width indicated in the project
instructions. Use a rotary cutter and straightedge to
obtain a straight cut. Remove the selvedges and join
the strips with diagonal seams.

CUTTING BIAS STRIPS

Cut strips to the width indicated in the project
instructions. Fold one cut end of the fabric to meet
one selvedge, forming a fold at a 45-degree angle
to the selvedge (**1**). With the fabric placed on a self-
healing mat, cut off the fold with a rotary cutter, using
a straight edge as a guide to make a straight cut. With
the straightedge and rotary cutter, cut strips to the
appropriate width (**2**). Join the strips with diagonal
seams.

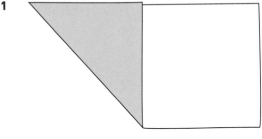

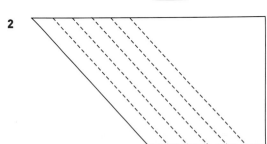

DIAGONAL SEAMS FOR JOINING STRIPS

Lay two strips right sides together, at right angles.
The area where the strips overlap forms a square.
Sew diagonally across the square as shown below.
Trim the excess fabric ¼" (6 mm) away from the seam
line and press the seam allowances open. Repeat to
join all the strips, forming one long fabric band.

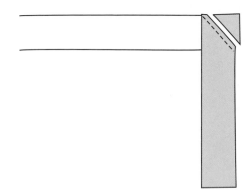

FOLD BINDING

A. Double-fold Binding This option will create binding
that is similar to packaged double-fold bias tape/
binding. Fold the strip in half lengthwise, with wrong
sides together; press. Open up the fold and then fold
each long edge toward the wrong side, so that the raw
edges meet in the middle (**1**). Refold the binding along
the existing center crease, enclosing the raw edges
(**2**), and press again.

B. Double-layer Binding This option creates a
double-thickness binding with only one fold. This
binding is often favored by quilters. Fold the strip in
half lengthwise with wrong sides together; press.

BINDING WITH MITERED CORNERS

*If using double-layer binding (option B, opposite page)
follow the alternate italicized instructions in parenthesis.*
Open the binding and press ½" (1.3 cm) to the wrong
side at one short end *(refold the binding at the center
increase and proceed)*. Starting with the folded-under
end of the binding, place it near the center of the
first edge of the project to be bound, matching the
raw edges, and pin in place. Begin sewing near the
center of one edge of the project, along the first
crease *(at the appropriate distance from the raw edge)*,
leaving several inches of the binding fabric free at the
beginning. Stop sewing ¼" (6 mm) before reaching
the corner, backtack, and cut the threads. Rotate the
project 90 degrees to position it for sewing the next
side. Fold the binding fabric up, away from the project,
at a 45-degree angle (**1**), then fold it back down along
the project raw edge (**2**). This forms a miter at the
corner. Stitch the second side, beginning at the project
raw edge (**2**) and ending ¼" (6 mm) from the next
corner, as before. Continue as established until you
have completed the last corner. Continue stitching
until you are a few inches from the beginning edge
of the binding fabric. Overlap the pressed beginning
edge of the binding by ½" (1.3 cm, or overlap more as
necessary for security) and trim the working edge to
fit. Finish sewing the binding *(opening the center fold
and tucking the raw edge inside the pressed end of the
binding strip)*. Refold the binding along all the creases
and then fold it over the project raw edges to the
back, enclosing the raw edges *(there are no creases
to worry about with option B)*. The folded edge of the
binding strip should just cover the stitches visible on
the project back. Slip stitch or blindstitch the binding
in place, tucking in the corners to complete the miters
as you go (**3**).

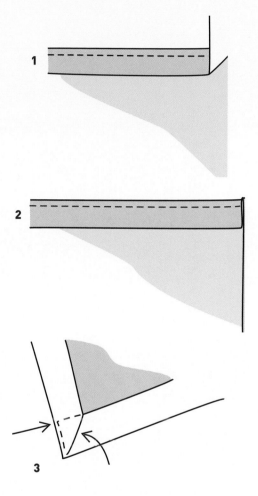

MEET THE *contributors*

BRETT BARA is the author of *Sewing in a Straight Line* (Potter Craft, 2011), editor of *Clever Crocheted Accessories* (Interweave, 2012), and host of the Emmy-nominated television series *Knit and Crochet Now!* She has written for numerous national magazines including *Marie Claire*, *Cosmopolitan*, *Details*, *Men's Health*, and *Prevention*. Brett blogs about crafts, DIY, and food at brettbara.com.

HEIDI BOYD is the author of fourteen craft books. Her most recent title is *Stitched Whimsy*. Heidi's goal is to make sophisticated design easy for everyone. She has a degree in fine arts and got her start as a contributor to *Better Homes & Gardens* publications. Heidi creates Whimsy Kits for handstitched felt woodland animals and lives in Maine with her husband and children. Heidi is a regular contributor to *Stitch* magazine and blogs at heidiboyd.blogspot.com.

STEFFANI K. BURTON has a B.A. in design from Arizona State University. She lives in Minnesota, where she works in her mother's fabric store as the third generation of women who sew in her family. Steffani's daily routine involves sewing, inspiring customers, creating quilts for clients, and designing store samples. She is passionate about sewing and design and shares her creative endeavors at sewwithsass.blogspot.com.

LISA COX is an occupational therapist by day and an avid crafter at night. Her designs have appeared in books and magazines including *Fabric by Fabric One Yard Wonders*, *Pretty Little Presents*, *Sweet Nothings*, *Craft Hope*, *Stitch*, *Quilting Arts Gifts*, *Homespun*, and *Handmade*. Lisa lives in Perth, Australia, and collaborates with her daughter on their Spoonful of Sugar Designs blog. Lisa blogs at spoonfulofsugardesigns.com.

MALKA DUBRAWSKY has a degree in studio art and works primarily as a fiber artist. Her work has been featured in exhibitions including Quilt National and Visions, and in publications including *Fiberarts: Design Book 7* (Lark Books, 2004). Malka's patterns have appeared in *Stitch* magazine and in a number of other quilting magazines and books. She is the author of *Color Your Cloth: A Quilter's Guide to Dyeing* (Lark Books, 2009) and *Fresh Quilting: Fearless Color, Design, and Inspiration* (Interweave, 2010). Malka blogs at stitchindye.blogspot.com.

RACHEL HAUSER is a self-taught sewist with a passion for color and modern design. She organizes an ever-growing quilting bee called Do Good Stitches that makes quilts for charities worldwide. A homeschooling mother of two who claims a modest homestead in South Carolina, Rachel is always stitching something lively and colorful. She blogs with a motto of "MAKE.handmade.do.Good" at stitchedincolor.com.

KEVIN KOSBAB is a freelance writer and designer whose patterns for quilts and sewing projects appear in magazines including *Stitch, American Patchwork and Quilting*, and *Quilter's World*. His book on appliqué for the modern quilter is scheduled for release in 2014 by Interweave. He lives in northern California with his partner and a handful of quadrupeds and produces modern patterns for creative quilters under the Feed Dog Designs label, available online at feeddog.net.

REBEKA LAMBERT (BEKI) lives with her husband and children in south Louisiana. She inherited her love of sewing from her mother and grandmother. Beki enjoys creating bags, purses, quilts, and her sewing pattern line. She has contributed to the *Pretty Little* series by Lark Books, *Craft Hope,* and *Stitch* magazine. The daily feedback and sharing of ideas through blogging keeps her inspired, so visit her online at artsycraftybabe.com.

APRIL MOFFATT comes from a long line of sewing divas. Her grandmother sewed her way through the Great Depression and her mother can sew just about anything. Today, April lives with her husband and four children in South Carolina, where she homeschools her children and designs sewing patterns for her own business and national publications. Visit her online at aprilmoffattdesigns.com.

MISSY SHEPLER is the co-author of *The Complete Idiot's Guide to Sewing* (Alpha Books, 2000). When possible, Missy combines her day job as a designer, author, and illustrator with her love of stitching by creating projects, patterns, and illustrations for sewing and quilting clients and publications. See what she's stitching up now at MissyStitches.com.

BLAIR STOCKER can most often be found in her bright basement studio, working with fabric, thrift-store spoils, or crochet hooks and yarn. She sells her original quilt patterns and remade vintage goods while also running Story Trading, a brand consulting company, with her husband Peter. Her children inspire her creativity every day. Blair writes about her creative pursuits on her Wise Craft blog at blairpeter.typepad.com.

AYUMI TAKAHASHI has loved making things from scratch throughout her childhood in Japan and adulthood in America; her favorite activities include sewing, cooking, herbal remedies, and making soaps and miniatures. Ayumi's sewing journey began with the gift of a sewing machine from her husband, and she has blogged about sewing and crafts since 2008 at her Pink Penguin blog. Ayumi is the author of *Patchwork, Please!* (Interweave, 2013). She lives with her husband Joe in Tokyo, Japan, and is online at ayumills.blogspot.com.

CAROL ZENTGRAF is a designer who specializes in sewing, fabrics, and decorating. She is an avid contributor to *Stitch* magazine as well as the author of *Pillows, Cushions, and Tuffets; Sewing for Outdoor Spaces;* and *Sewing Season's Greetings.* She lives in Peoria, Illinois.